ALSO BY JENNIFER COHEN

Badass Body Goals: The Booty Building and Waist Trimming Journal

Strong Is the New Skinny: How to Eat, Live, and Move to Maximize Your Power

No Gym Required: Unleash Your Inner Rock Star

BIGGE
BETTE
BOLDE

BIGGER, BETTER, BOLDER

Live the Life You Want, Not the Life You Get

Jennifer Cohen

hachette
BOOKS   New York

Hachette Go, an imprint of Hachette Books
Hachette Book Group
1290 Avenue of the Americas
New York, NY 10104
HachetteGo.com
Facebook.com/HachetteGo
Instagram.com/HachetteGo

First Edition: December 2022

Hachette Books is a division of Hachette Book Group, Inc.

The Hachette Go and Hachette Books name and logos are trademarks of Hachette Book Group, Inc.

The publisher is not responsible for websites (or their content) that are not owned by the publisher.

Print book interior design by Jeff Williams

Library of Congress Cataloging-in-Publication Data

Name: Cohen, Jennifer, author.
Title: Bigger, better, bolder: live the life you want, not the life you get / Jennifer Cohen.
Description: New York, NY: Hachette Go, [2022] | Includes bibliographical references.
Identifiers: LCCN 2022019165 | ISBN 9780306829581 (hardcover) | ISBN 9780306829598 (paperback) | ISBN 9780306829604 (ebook)
Subjects: LCSH: Self-actualization (Psychology) | Self-esteem. |Self-confidence.
Classification: LCC BF637.S4 C6514 2022 | DDC 158.1—dc23/eng/20220825
LC record available at https://lccn.loc.gov/2022019165

ISBNs: 978-0-306-82958-1 (hardcover), 978-0-306-82960-4 (ebook)

Printed in the United States of America

LSC-C

Printing 1, 2022

To my two bold children, Dylan and Sydney.
Keep asking, reaching, and chasing
for bigger, bolder, and better now
and forever. Mommy loves you both more
than anything in the world.

Contents

Contents

My Promise to You

I know what it takes to get what you want in life.

It's a habit that anyone can learn, a skill you can develop, a gift you don't need to be born with.

It's the key to unlocking success.

I discovered its power when I was a girl in a small town, chasing a big dream.

I will teach it to you, step-by-step, in the 16 Principles in this book.

I'll coach you as you practice this. I'll help you get back up again when you fall.

I'll motivate you to keep going, even when you get knocked down and want to give up.

Because even when you fail, you'll start to feel stronger with each try you make.

The more experience you get, the more confident you'll be.

And then one day, you'll start to get good at it. Really good.

If you make it a habit starting right now, if you practice, if you keep going even when you fail,

I guarantee that eventually you will get what you want—at work, at home,

virtually everywhere your life unfolds.

It takes work but it's worth the effort.

I practice this skill every day in my continued pursuit of a bigger, better, bolder life filled with fascinating people, places, and things.

I consider this skill to be my superpower. Here it is:

I am bold.

I take action.

I chase what I want, instead of taking what I can get.

Be bold with me. It works. And it really will change your life.

—Jennifer Cohen

Introduction

NO MATTER HOW YOU'VE SPENT the last few years, whether you were able to work from home, were still in school, struggled finding employment, or headed to your in-person job each day, there is no denying that the global pandemic was one hell of a wake-up call, and the alarm still seems to be going off. The world changed forever, and the old cliché proved true: turns out life really *is* short. But as we settle into what now passes for normal, how many people will go back to settling for what they have, even if it's not enough? And how many will listen to that little voice that urges them to go after what they really want?

After everything we've been through, why settle for what you can get, instead of chasing what you truly want?

Ask yourself: What do you want *most* in life? And why don't you have it?

I'm going to help you answer those questions, and then I'm going to show you how to go after what you want, with a promise that you will eventually get it if you follow my lead. And if you don't get exactly that one thing? Well, you may wind up with something much better—maybe something that you never even knew existed.

Before we dive deeper, for the purposes of this discussion let's focus on the meaning of "want" and "things." I'm not referring to a burning desire for a flashy car or an indulgence like a luxe vacation. If that's what you're after, put this book down and pick up your credit card, because there's always someone ready to take your money. This may be a book about getting what you want, but it's not a book about getting all the material things and money that you desire. This isn't a get-rich-quick book. It's a make-your-*life*-rich book.

When I ask what "things" you "want," I'm referring to those intangibles that enrich our lives, like new and interesting experiences, satisfying relationships, and the ability to become who we believe we are meant to be. I'm talking about the things you want right now and others you've yet to discover. A bigger, better, bolder life is filled with rich experiences—and zero regrets.

Why don't we chase what we desire most? It's because we're stuck in the good-enough trap. At some point we start to live our lives by default, taking whatever we can get. We get used to a so-so state of affairs, whether we're talking personal or professional, because it's "good enough." *It's OK.*

It'll do. Besides, if I ask for something better, if I try to change this, if I go for what I really want, it might not happen. I could lose what I already have. So, what I have in front of me, it will do. It's good enough.

The good enough mindset is fueled by fear and self-doubt—by thinking that you'll fail if you reach for something you really want, that you'll be rejected, that someone will tell you no, that it's just too hard to pull off. So yeah, it's easier to take what you can get and avoid the disappointment and humiliation of missing your target. That's why you don't act. But not taking those chances—not asking, not trying, not deciding to go for it—is going to cost you, because settling for good enough never leads to something better.

Good enough is how we wind up with relationships that sputter out or grow toxic. Good enough is why we stay in crappy jobs that don't pay us what we're worth. Good enough is why we let our physical health go and our spirits sink. Good enough is why we don't take action to get what we want, and why we are content to remain complacent with what we have.

Screw good enough. That's no way to go through this one life we're given. Instead of good, go for better. Instead of what you get, go for bigger. Instead of fearing failure, be bold—and then be bolder.

When you become bold, good things start to happen. Then better things start to happen. You break free from what's holding you back, you aren't afraid to fail, and you learn from every shot you take, even when you miss the target—*especially* when you miss the target. And you definitely bust out of the good enough trap.

When you become bold, you ask for what you want—and more often than not you get it.

Why You Should Take Advice from a Former Olive Garden Employee

I know exactly how it feels to go from settling to chasing after what I really want—and getting it. It was worth it, but it took a lot of trying, a lot (*a lot*) of failing, and it's a never-ending process. I still work at it, every single day. I've been in your shoes, taking what life handed to me before I grew bold enough to chase what I wanted, and sometimes I still slip those old shoes on. But they're not broken in—they're just broken.

Becoming comfortable with failure was an early lesson for me growing up, starting with school, where I struggled academically. I was regularly sent to the "resource teacher" for extra tutoring just so I could keep up. One day, my mom told me that my teacher said I was "average, at best." Mom wasn't trying to hurt my feelings, but *average at best*? Ouch. Not only was I not keeping up in school, not only was I not keeping up with my family's standards of academic success, but I was barely average. At *best*.

I could stand to be just about anything but . . . average? To me, "average" translated to "good enough," and good enough wasn't good enough for me. That teacher's brutal assessment of my intelligence (just my book smarts, as it turns out) at such a young age lit the proverbial fire under my butt. Starting then, I made up for my lackluster grades with grit and determination.

Not being able to rely on straight As (or even Bs . . . or sometimes Cs . . .) meant I had to hone my skills in other areas, so I figured out what I *was* good at early on: trying, persevering, getting comfortable with failing so that I wasn't afraid to go back and try again. One game-changing lesson I learned early on was this: If I wanted something—particularly something that seemed to come so easily to others around me—I would have to ask for it. And when people told me no, I would have to ask for it *again*. And again, and again, and again . . . until I got a win. And guess what? I got really good at asking! Asking and failing and asking again is the foundation of boldness.

When I was twelve, I desperately wanted to earn my own money (and not by babysitting, the default), so I marched into the Olive Garden restaurant near my house and asked for a job as a hostess. The manager laughed, explaining I was way too young for that position, and because of our liquor laws I wasn't even old enough to work where alcohol was served. To get around this, I suggested he hire me to work *outside*, where I would greet patrons and open the door. "No, that's not a job for a kid!" the manager said.

But I didn't give up. I came back after school the next day and asked if he'd reconsider. "No." I went back again the next day. "No." And I went back again . . . until finally

I wore him down and he hired me as the Olive Garden Door Opener and Greeter. I was not allowed to go past the restaurant's entrance due to the liquor laws, but I held that door open, smiled brightly, and greeted my customers like I owned the place. And I got the better-than-babysitting paycheck I wanted.

A few years later, I would take a career skills assessment test in high school. The results suggested that with my record, my best bet at career success was to become a forest ranger. That's not to say that being a forest ranger doesn't take skill and intelligence, but in Canada, where I grew up, apparently it didn't require those elusive good grades. Clearly, the universe was still hell-bent on telling me, "Don't get your hopes up." I did anyway! I was always working on some scheme to keep myself moving forward, no matter how crazy it might have seemed to just about anyone else. My mom would say I was like "a squirrel always looking for a nut." I was always chasing better. Something bigger. I've been looking for those nuts my entire life.

Like the teacher who pronounced me "average, at best," that lousy assessment test was yet another pivotal moment in my life, perhaps *the* pivotal moment. I was a young adult by then, not just a pesky kid who wanted spending money. I knew that college and the "real world" were on the horizon. And when I took that test and got those results, I finally understood that I did not have to settle for whatever life (or life's career-assessment-test designers) handed me. I may not have had ideal grades, but I had determination and perseverance. Even if my dreams were still coming into focus at that young age, I had bigger, better, and bolder aspirations for myself.

I gradually learned something else, too, and I rethought my distaste of being labeled average. It turns out "average, at best" could be turned into an asset. Mediocrity, as you will learn, can work for you, not against you.

After graduating high school, I earned a bachelor's degree in psychology and topped that off with a master's in sports management. Yes, I had to work harder than my college classmates, but by then I'd had years of practice! I would go on to land jobs with the National Basketball Association, several major record labels, and a media-training firm, among others. And eventually I found my niche in the fitness industry, writing best-selling books, creating a weight-tracking app, launching a fitness shoe that celebrities loved, and working with music and movie stars, and with world-famous athletes as well.

As a trainer, I helped all my clients up their game, from the glitterati I trained in person to the everyday people who wore my shoes and worked out to my DVDs or read my books. The goal was the same for all of them: not just to improve their physical performance but to strengthen their mindset as well. And now I'm going to help you.

I've found joy and success helping people set goals they can reach, motivating them, helping them grow stronger and hit their targets through good habits, healthy practices, and hard work that pays off. But the lessons I impart have never been limited to improving only the body. They train the brain as well. My clients take their newfound strengths—physical and mental—into the real world. They become bold.

I'm the host of a weekly podcast, *Habits & Hustle*, where my guests are a fantastic mix of entrepreneurs, best-selling authors, thought leaders, and visionaries across a range of fields. My show, and my obsessive curiosity, has enabled me to study how extremely successful people set goals and reach them—how they get what they want, what makes them successful, and what makes them happy.

To a person, one thing always holds true: All my guests have faced rejection and failure at some point on their journey, but they acted and reacted with boldness. They just keep asking, keep trying, keep changing, and keep tweaking until they get what they want—or they find another opportunity, a better one, that they didn't even know existed. It's what I've done, and it's what you can do too. (The story of how I wound up with a top-ranked podcast is in itself a story of failure and then acting with boldness—it was supposed to be a network TV show—but I'll save that for later.)

What's the Worst That Can Happen?

In addition to embracing failure and using it to propel you forward, it helps if you ask yourself a game-changing question—the same one I asked myself as a teenager growing up in the sleepy city of Winnipeg, Manitoba, when I'd set my sights on my dream job. I wanted to be a VJ, a "video jockey"—remember those?—on Canada's version of MTV, and producers were welcoming local talent to apply. But I needed one essential thing to get an audition: a killer demo tape, with me on camera, interviewing people like a seasoned pro. Hmm. By that point in my young life, I had bravado, I had chutzpah, and I had grit—but I had *no clue* how to make a demo tape!

I was more than a little afraid to take a shot at my biggest dream ever. Despite my scrappy personality, I was still a bit of an awkward small-town kid. But then again, by that time I was comfortable with failure. I'd had plenty of practice and I knew that if a door was closed, it paid off to look for a window—and one day I spotted one that was cracked open just enough.

I dreamed up a plot to get that killer demo tape—a plan that involved the family video camera, my best imitation of a celebrity interviewer with her own show, and my ability to corral a super-famous Hollywood star who happened to be visiting my hometown. I was right on the brink of carrying out my plan, but I was oh-so-scared of blowing it.

I hesitated. I agonized. I thought of all the reasons why my plan would flop. And then I asked myself this question that turned it all around: *What's the worst that can happen?* Turns out, I had nothing to lose, and everything to gain. But I'll tell you more about my Keanu Moment (yes, *that* Keanu) later.

When I was approached a while back to do a TEDx talk on being bold, which would be taped for online viewing,

I admit to being a little nervous, as the format was all new to me. What if I was immortalized on camera for internet posterity and I looked and sounded like a tongue-tied dope? What if I became a bad meme? But when I asked myself that all-important question—*Jennifer, what's the worst that can happen?*—I realized I had absolutely nothing to lose by sharing my experiences and my lessons on boldness. And millions of YouTube views later, it turns out a lot of people had much to gain.

My TEDx talk was built around the transformative power of boldness, and why I think it's the strongest predictor of success—more so than intelligence. Smart people are good at many things, but unfortunately one of those "talents" is overthinking all the ways something or someone will fail. Bold people, on the other hand, think of all the good things that will happen when things go right. I'm not saying that smart people can't be bold, or that bold people aren't intelligent. But when it comes to getting what you want? It's boldness—not brain power, connections, or money—that's the secret sauce.

Almost immediately after that talk, I knew I'd delivered a major message that resonated across a wide range of ages and professions. Besides the requests for formal speaking engagements (from the country's top business schools like MIT, Harvard, Wharton, and Columbia, from Fortune 500 companies, and from many others), I have fielded thousands of requests from everyday people who have wanted to know more: *How can I chase what I want? How can I be bold?*

That's when I knew I had to write this book and share the 16 Principles you're about to read, all designed to set you on your journey for a bigger, better, bolder life. This is the ultimate guide for chasing what you want, not taking what you can get.

Ready? Set? Bold!

Principle by Principle, you're going to learn how to reset your mind and prime yourself to be bold. Here's a taste of what's ahead.

Principle #1: Strive for Bigger and Better

Principle #2: Discover Your Bold Type

Principle #3: You Gotta Believe

Principle #4: Change Your Mind

Principle #5: Practice Bold Habits

Principle #6: Don't Stop Before You Start

Principle #7: Choose a Direction, Not a Destination

Principle #8: Be Obsessively Curious

Principle #9: Naivete Is a Strength

Principle #10: Mediocrity Is a Superpower

Principle #11: Bundle Your Bold

Principle #12: Fix It, Farm It Out, Forget It

Principle #13: Ask for What You Want

Principle #14: Be Bold, Not Smart

Principle #15: The 10 Percent Target

Principle #16: Bold Is for Life

You'll find a useful tool at the very end of this book—The 16 Principles Workbook—designed to help you personalize and explore each Principle one at a time and to reinforce everything you're about to read. (I suggest you wait until you've read through the entire book before you use the workbook, though if you feel you need a little extra help with a specific Principle, you can flip to the back and focus on it.) You can write your answers in the space provided or use a separate journal if you want to write more.

Throughout these Principles, I'll be your coach. I've already shared that as a fitness trainer, my job was never limited to helping clients build up their physical strength. Everything starts in your brain. You can do a lot more squats if you have the right mindset. But if you aren't mentally bringing it, you won't be able to do a single one.

I start with the brain, not the body, because I've always approached physical training from a mental angle. Before I received numerous certifications as a trainer, I earned a degree in psychology—and I would have pursued psychology as a profession if I hadn't fallen in love with the work I do now, motivating people from the inside out.

I've helped thousands—from famous names to ordinary men and women—set realistic goals, build up their strength, and learn how to maintain their newfound levels of fitness. But in every instance—whether the goal was 20 pounds or 120 pounds, whether I was training a star like Christina Aguilera, an athlete like Dennis Rodman, or a regular person who used my workout app, books, or DVDs—success hinged on having the right mindset, on knowing how to push through the failures and make progress through incremental changes, and on getting up and trying again the next day if they missed their targets. Building up that muscle in the mind has always been part of my job.

Building up your "bold muscle," as you can think of it, works much the same way. You start by figuring out what you want, and then you begin to take action through small, doable steps. You build up your skill, you practice, you get confident, you fail, but you go back and do it again till you get what you're chasing.

Bold people come in all shapes and sizes and ages and have different definitions of personal success. Some are famous and have houses on both coasts, some live right next door to you. One may have happily handed you your morning coffee. Another may be sitting in the corner office at your company. One bold person may host a talk show, while another did the host's makeup. But beneath the surface, bold people have one thing in common: they don't stop trying, even when they fail. If they can't go through the door, they go through the window. It's what I've done, and it's what you can do too. Let me show you how.

PART 1
GETTING TO BOLD

Principle #1

Strive for Bigger and Better

HAPPINESS IS LIKE SAILING ON the ocean with the people you love, until you realize how deep the water is, and then look toward the distant horizon and start praying no one rocks the damned boat. (Don't hold your breath—something or someone always rocks the boat.)

I'm not trying to talk you out of striving for happiness, but I do want you to think about what "finding happiness" means to some of us. It's contentment, true. It's being satisfied, for a while anyway. It's about getting things that you think you want, or that other people want for you. But happiness, all too often, is about being content with the status quo, being satisfied with what's in front of you, even if it's not what you truly want. If you find yourself saying, "But I'm finally happy!" and you're barely twenty-five or you're turning sixty-five—well, *then* what?

I find it ironic that the stock image of happiness often involves a cheery, sturdy, white picket fence. A fence keeps you safe. A fence lets the world know you feel safe. But a fence also closes you in. A fence keeps others out. A fence stops you from chasing what you really want beyond your fenced-in world.

Fences get old. They need new coats of paint. They warp. They need repair. They do their best to stand erect until a bad storm comes and knocks them down.

Happiness is good enough until a storm comes along.

Some people choose to rebuild their fence. After all, they were happy before the storm came. But some people see an opportunity to grow, to let go of all the physical and psychological barriers keeping them from discovering what's on the other side of their damn fence. They're the bold ones.

Happiness is a destination. Boldness is a direction.

A Bold Life Is a Rich Life

This book isn't about finding happiness. There's an endless supply of great self-help books that will help you with that. Instead, *Bigger, Better, Bolder* is about finding a richer, fuller life. It's about acknowledging that a good enough life is not the same as a good life.

To be clear, I don't mean "rich" in terms of a big fat bank account—not that doing something financially rewarding is a bad idea. But the thing about focusing on the money and only the money is that it's never enough. Because there will always be someone who has more wealth and affluence. A better car. A nicer house. A higher white picket fence.

The rich life I want for you is known by experts as the "psychologically rich" life. It essentially means a life that is rich with fulfilling experiences and relationships, not just stuff. A rich life is filled with leaps and bounds, not timid steps or no forward motion. The person who leads a rich life is always ready for the next adventure, big or small. A rich life is about variety, not indifference; about newness and change, about discovery and self-discovery. It's about collecting interesting places, people, and experiences—bigger, better, bolder experiences.

The psychologically rich life isn't about seeking comfort and security. It's not about being satisfied or satisfying others. Some people spend their lives keeping in line. Being politically correct. Never taking risks. Not standing up for what they believe, or what they know, or what they want, or who they are meant to be. And for some, that's a good enough life.

But it's not a rich life. Strive for a rich life. Be bold.

- Bold people push the limits. Others are stymied by limited thinking.

- Bold people break through the system. Others are subject to conformity.

- Bold people take action to move the needle. Others remain stuck, resistant to change.

- Bold people go for it. Others go with the flow.

- Bold people create opportunity. Others wait for something to happen.

- Bold people seek novelty. Others are OK with the same old, same old.

- Bold people are curious and interested in other people. Others mind their own business.

- Bold people accept rejection. Others live with regret.

- Bold people get comfortable with failure. Others fear failure and never try.

- Bold people have big stories to tell. Others live vicariously through those stories.

Is Your Brain Stopping You from Being Bold?

Bold people dare to leap without overthinking. But you may think, "That's not smart! Look before you leap!" So, here's the catch with "look before you leap," which I touched on in the first few pages of this book. Smart people think of all the ways things can go wrong before they make a move that could change their lives and get them what they want. Smart people know all the ways they can fail. But bold people think of all ways things will go right. Bold people know that, win or lose, they've succeeded by trying. (And note: I didn't say bold people leap without thinking. I said they leap without *over*thinking!)

Bold people can be very smart, but they must also be willing to be stupid. That is, to be naive. To be open. To learn from failure, which is always a real possibility. But smart people who are afraid to be considered ignorant believe they can slay the beast with intelligence. They did their research. They are rational. They are going to just stop for a second and consult their pros and cons list, and then pour that data into a spreadsheet. And wait a few more weeks until the stock market settles or make another call to confirm something or take one more precaution because they absolutely cannot risk failure.

And that's how smart people overthink taking action, while bold people are already in the ring, fighting for what they want.

Climb That Tree

Remember when you were growing up and there was that kid? You know, the one who always wanted to do stuff like climb the tree in the neighbor's yard, even though some kids said, "No way! It's too high! You'll never get to the top! You'll get in so much trouble!" while others (or sometimes the same kids) chanted, "Do it! Do it! Do it!" and egged the daredevil onward and upward. That kid proudly climbed nearly all the way to the top, only to realize they had no idea how to get down. But they eventually figured it out. And yes, they got some cuts and bruises along the way. Maybe even a broken bone. Maybe they did get in trouble. But as soon as they could, that kid would climb right back up the same damn tree. They'd get even higher this time. And they'd get back down even faster. Eventually they'd get to the top! All the kids would celebrate their bravery. Where did that kid's courage come from? Where did their fearlessness come from?

That kid never feared the climb. They just climbed.

Maybe that kid was you. Maybe it was the kid you aspired to be. Either way, as we get older, it's hard to remember how to be so fearless.

Here's a tip as you strive to be bold: *Be that kid.*

Were you the kind of kid determined to be in the school musical, even though you couldn't dance, carry a tune, or remember your lines? Sure, they put you in the back row of the chorus and only gave you two lines, which you flubbed. But you had a blast! Your friends laughed and clapped! You got to be onstage, which is what you wanted!

Be that kid.

Did you watch ice skating during the Winter Olympics and think, "I could do that!" even though you didn't know how to ice skate? You went to the rink, strapped on some rented skates, got on the ice, and promptly fell on your ass. And it kinda hurt! But . . . you still liked it, so you got up and tried again. And you fell on your ass again, but you were hooked. You even got your mom to buy you your own skates. You got better, but still you fell on your butt. And you got up and tried again. Stand up, skate, fall, stand up, repeat—and now you were skating a little longer and falling a little less. When the rink closed, you packed up your skates and grinned because you couldn't wait to get back on the ice and fall on your ass the next week.

Be that kid.

When I was that kid, I'd embarrass my mother by asking her friends probing questions about how they made their money, if they liked going to work or hated their job, how much their house cost—the types of questions well-mannered children don't ask of adults. But I was curious about how the grown-up world worked. I wanted information and I got it. I was fearless. I was bold.

I'm still that kid.

What we don't know to fear, we don't fear. Kids know this. Bold people know this. They know they may get hurt or fail or get a no. But that's what it means to take risks and to try. And yes, it's possible to be bold in some areas and not so bold in others. Personally, I was scared to climb trees! I was definitely one of the kids on the ground, cheering on the daredevil. But I had no problem asking my mom's friends blunt questions that I'm sure other kids were too shy (or polite!) to ask, despite their curiosity.

23

Boldness is important when you're going after what you authentically want, not what others want for you. So feeling pressured to go downhill skiing on a black diamond trail if you'd rather relax in front of the fire and meet up later isn't about being bold or fearful. It's a matter of *doing what you want to do*. (Swap out downhill skiing for taking a "safe" corporate job you don't want though everyone says you're crazy not to do it for the money, versus accepting a less lucrative but interesting position at a nonprofit you love.) Remember this: chasing what you want takes boldness, and so does standing up for what you want, especially when others want something else for you.

Without risk there is no reward. For bold people, taking risks *is* the reward. With every try, we are one step closer to getting what we want. Because with each scab from a skinned knee, each cheer from friends down on the ground or out in the audience, we become more resilient.

We become that kid.

Principle #2

Discover Your Bold Type

MANY PEOPLE ASSUME THAT YOU have to be *born* bold, and if you weren't, then tough luck—you will never be bold. That's just not true. The bigger, better, bolder life is accessible to everyone because boldness is a skill one learns and develops just like any other. And like all skills, you have to practice it.

If you want to get stronger, you don't go to the gym once and call it a day. If you want to learn a new language, you don't take a couple of classes and declare yourself fluent. And if you want to run a marathon, you don't jog around the block and assume you're ready to run 26.2 miles.

To acquire a new skill, you learn it, you practice it, and you work your way to becoming better at it. And the more you practice, the better you get. It's the same for boldness— a skill you can learn. And the more you practice becoming bolder, the bolder you will become.

Born That Way? Most of Us Aren't

Do you feel like you're going backward here? If you were "that kid" once upon a time, do you worry that you're becoming more risk averse as time goes by, with age and experience? Are you becoming more comfortable settling for what you've got, rather than chasing what you want?

Or maybe you think it's just not part of your personality and who you were born to be. Your mom is bold, and so is your sister, but you're more like your dad, who is on the shy, quiet side.

Still, boldness isn't like height or eye color, programmed in the womb (colored contacts aside). New research shows that while 50 percent of our personality traits are inherited, the other 50 percent is within our control to change, learn, and develop. Which is a good thing, since research also shows that 90 percent of us *want* to change some aspect of our personality.

His Tastes Changed (Literally)— and So Did His Personality

Depending on your age, you may have already noticed some personality changes, which is natural as we mature or when we go through life-changing experiences, including trauma or sudden changes in circumstances. Sometimes we adapt our personalities when we enter certain types of relationships, or we behave differently when we take on a new job with more responsibility.

We likely don't even realize how we've changed until we look back. Usually when our personalities change, an event or another person inspires the transformation. Maybe you used to be the life of the party, you savored your lazy weekends, and you didn't grocery shop until you had nothing in the fridge but a bottle of rosé. You were super laid-back about domestic life, and it was all fine—until you and your partner started a family. Now you're super organized, you meal plan, and, while you still love seeing your friends, you only socialize if you can be in bed by ten. (Even better, 9:30—who am I kidding?)

Relationships can trigger personality changes—including positive ones that can make you bolder. Take my friend Greg, for example, who was never terribly adventurous with food. He was a creature of habit who preferred to go to the same handful of restaurants, where he'd order the same dishes without variation. At home, he cooked and ate the same small variety of foods. When some of Greg's friends would tease him about having the palate of a preschooler, he'd always say, "Why change? The food I like is just fine."

But then Greg got into a serious relationship with a woman who adored trying new restaurants, dining on exotic cuisine, and seeking out the latest food trends. At first, Greg agreed to try these unfamiliar restaurants, as well as food trucks and farmers' markets, because it made his girlfriend happy. But over time, Greg realized that he really enjoyed these new tastes and experiences. He got hooked on seeking out different locales and dishes. Greg was becoming a foodie!

It's been nearly a year since Greg and his ex broke up, and instead of going back to his same old haunts, he's been inviting his friends to join him at new restaurants he's heard about, from dives to white-tablecloth establishments. He scans the food section in the paper, reads reviews, and hangs out at the farmers' market to see what's new. He is hooked on cooking shows and loves trying out new recipes. And now when he's teased about his 180, Greg's response is: "Hey, anyone can change."

It Could Happen to You

Greg got a boost from a romantic partner who gradually led him to change his personality and become more open and adventurous and less rigid and set in his ways. But if it hadn't been for his omnivorous ex, could he have changed voluntarily? The answer is yes. Even without an outside influence, you can change. Sure, another person or a life event can give you a push, but in the field of psychology, experts have long agreed that it is possible to change your personality voluntarily.

Still, it takes a lot more than the desire, intention, or even belief that you can change. You have to act like it. That is, you have to *take on* those personality traits as if you'd always had them and engage in actions that reinforce those traits. Personality expert and psychologist Nathan Hudson and his research team at Southern Methodist University found that when people made the decision to change a personality trait—specifically, one of the overarching traits referred to in personality psychology as "the Big Five" (listed below)—those who successfully completed specific tasks associated with those traits were successful and saw the desired changes in their personalities.

The Big Five Personality Traits

- Openness to experience (curious versus cautious)

- Conscientiousness (organized versus careless)

- Extraversion (outgoing versus reserved)

- Agreeableness (friendly versus critical)

- Neuroticism (sensitive versus confident)

Take a look at "openness to experience" and consider my menu-challenged friend Greg. He engaged in tasks that took him from cautious to curious. Hudson and his researchers predicted that so long as a person in search of change keeps practicing, the personality change will become even more ingrained.

In other words: The more action you take to change your personality, the more your personality will change. And the more you keep at it, the more it'll stick. With this approach, it doesn't matter if you are starting from scratch or you got 50 percent of your mom's boldness.

While boldness isn't technically one of the Big Five, it is associated with a few of the traits. Think of boldness as a cocktail of high extraversion (outgoing) and low neuroticism (confident). Boldness also requires more than a dash of openness to experience, including curiosity, inventiveness, and creativity. Add in a helping of conscientiousness (you're prepared but you don't overthink it) and agreeableness (you're not a jerk, which means others will help you when you need it).

The Big Five is the basis for a popular personality test. You can try any one of the many free online quizzes if you want to get a little more insight on your personality, which might be useful as it relates to your current level of boldness (try this free version at *FiveThirtyEight*: https://projects .fivethirtyeight.com/personality-quiz/#). You can gauge how your personality has changed from where you once were, to where you are today, to where you'll be once you complete the Bold Moves tasks throughout the book. A Big Five quiz can help you discover if you're already leaning into extraversion but your levels of neuroticism are above average. Are you on the lower end of openness to experience, or is that a personality trait where you get a high score? Where can you flex some of the bold muscles you already have, and what traits need more of a workout? (Incidentally, you don't have to be a full-on extravert to be bold. But it's beneficial to borrow from that personality trait if you need to boost your level of bold.)

Choose Your Bold

I've broken down boldness into two categories or directions that you can move in: social boldness and self-actualization boldness. Both can serve you in living a richer life, and by no means do you have to choose just one. In fact, I encourage you to become bolder in every area of life you'd like to enrich. That overarching approach is the key to a richer life, after all. Plus, each area where you choose to make bold moves will have a positive effect on your readiness to begin making bold moves in other areas.

Social boldness is about getting what you want in dating and romantic relationships, in marriage and parenthood, with family and friends, in your career, in your community at large, and in your ability to lead others toward what you value most. Social boldness is about making deeper connections in your personal relationships and stronger and more productive networks for work.

Self-actualization boldness is about becoming who you truly believe you are meant to be; it's about striving toward reaching your potential. This type of transformation can happen creatively, like finally writing that novel you've been thinking about or inventing the next big thing. Or you may want to push yourself with extreme performance activities like climbing Mount Kilimanjaro.

Self-actualization boldness may be just what you need to emerge from a dark point in your life or a time of great change due to unforeseen circumstances. It's for when you are ready to explore all that life offers, or you're tired of the same old, same old and want to shake things up. And I'm a big fan of shaking things up. You can't grow if you don't take action.

So, where do you want to stretch your bold muscles first—or most?

Do you want to become bolder at work and ask for that promotion you know you deserve? Or are you looking to change your career altogether and become an entrepreneur? Do you want to become more confident in dating and relationships? Perhaps you want to be less timid in social situations and make new friends while moving away from the bad influences who've kept you from living a healthier lifestyle. If you can relate to these issues, a focus on social boldness is a good place to begin.

Are you ready for an adventure? Do you want to learn how to surf, or pilot your own plane, or jump out of one? Are you an explorer who wants to discover new places, people, and experiences? Are you feeling unstoppable and ready to take on physical challenges that no one expects you to achieve, let alone try? Do you want to take your singer-songwriter skills to the recording studio? Do you want to paint? Sculpt? Write a novel or a book of poetry? Are you an inventor with great ideas to better the world that you're eager to put into action? Then self-actualization boldness is your primary focus.

Or, perhaps these examples are too big and bold for you today, and you're simply looking to no longer feel like a doormat at home, or you're an empty nester trying to figure out your next step, or you want to feel more confident with how you look and feel. It doesn't matter. The Principles in this book work no matter how you want to make your life bigger, better, and bolder.

I truly believe there is no stopping anyone who yearns to be bold. You may have practical reasons why you can't embark on sailing around the world right now, but that doesn't mean you can't begin to practice for your journey by becoming bolder through negotiating with the roofer, asking for a raise, standing up for a cause you believe in, and getting more comfortable not getting what you want, because you'll become more resilient for having tried.

Practice now, because when you're ready to set sail, you'll have all the bold skills you need to launch you on your way.

PART 2

BUILD YOUR BOLD

Principle #3

You Gotta Believe

IT TAKES PRACTICE TO DEVELOP the skills for becoming a virtuoso musician, a champion athlete, or top-notch entrepreneur. It takes hard work. It takes commitment. It takes tenacity and resilience, particularly after the inevitable failure and rejection. And for anyone who reaches those lofty heights, whatever they may be, it takes something else: belief in one's self.

You may not be aiming for Olympic gold or a spot on the Fortune 500—but to be bold, you too must believe in yourself. That's the starting point on our journey to boldness. You need to believe that you are bold, no matter how far from bold you may be feeling right now.

When I say you need to believe, I don't mean you should do it by muttering empty affirmations in front of the mirror when you are brushing your teeth in the morning, especially if you're rolling your eyes and thinking, "Yeah, like this BS is gonna work."

There is a better way than talking to yourself in the bathroom, though affirmations (done with the right attitude) can be powerful. But here's how you tweak it: it isn't just about belief; it's about identity. If you can identify as a bold person—and you'll do it through practice, practice, practice, just like all those world-class musicians and athletes—you'll be taking a giant leap toward getting what you want in life.

The Science of Bold

In the world of psychology, self-efficacy is a key idea in social cognitive theory, and the quick-and-dirty definition is that if you believe you are capable, you can get stuff done. The concept of self-efficacy originated from research by Albert Bandura, PhD, an influential expert in psychology whose findings have persisted since the 1960s.

According to Dr. Bandura, self-efficacy is "the belief in one's capabilities to organize and execute the courses of action required to manage prospective situations." In other words, it's having the belief in your ability to do the work required to achieve your goals of getting what you want in life. Or, as I'd put it to you:

- Believe you *can* get the shit done.

- Believe you *will* get the shit done.

- Then *get* the shit done.

And you will get closer and closer to getting what you want. (Also, saying those three things out loud is a lot more fun and satisfying than looking in the mirror and saying to your reflection, "I believe in you!" Try it out.)

People with self-efficacy have agency. They believe they have control over their lives: their social environment, level of motivation, dedication to performance, and emotional well-being. That's because they believe that when they focus on achieving goals through bold habits, behavior, and actions, they're doing everything within their control to win. They perceive challenges and roadblocks as things to master or conquer, not avoid or feel deflated and defeated by. They don't take failure personally; failure is an opportunity to get back out there and find another way in, through, or around.

Of course, even the best-laid plans don't guarantee absolute success, no matter how hard we try. But people with healthy levels of self-efficacy believe they can and will persevere when the going gets tough—another benefit. They determine how they perceive the situation. Yep, you're in charge of how you interpret what transpires. Lose a business deal? It's a loss; you're not a loser.

OK, it's time to practice believing in yourself. Remember that being bold is a skill. It doesn't matter whether you're a rank beginner or intermediate or advanced (and even then, just like the pros, you have to keep practicing—bold is for life). Lay your bold foundation, or strengthen what you've already started to build, with these steps.

Become a Master of One

The best and simplest way to begin to believe you're bold is to complete one small, bold task from start to finish. Today's task is to ask for one small thing that you want, instead of taking what you get. Like weight training to build muscle, the task should be uncomfortable enough that your bold muscles begin to develop strength, but not so painful that you never want to try it again.

Small is relative, so I suggest bold beginners start by asking for something that is just a step above your comfort level. Completing this task will build confidence and help you become more comfortable asking for bigger things down the road. And for those of you feeling like you're beyond asking for a refill on the free iced tea, then go for it—ask for something bigger.

Your big, bold baby step can be as basic as asking for extra ketchup, a slice of lemon for your water, or a sharper knife for your steak when you're at a restaurant. You can ask that friend who watches all those home organization shows to come over and help you organize your closets—she's always offering, but you have been hesitant to take her up on it, as you don't want to "impose." Call the cable company or your cell phone provider or your mortgage company to negotiate a better deal. Ask your boss if you can be a part of the team she is putting together for the new client project you're dying to work on.

```
┌─────────────────────────────────────────────┐
│                BOLD MOVE                      │
│                                               │
│  Don't overthink it! It's just one small task.│
│  Pick something and go for it.                │
└─────────────────────────────────────────────┘
```

Be a Copycat

Watching people you admire or you relate to do something you've never dared to try can increase your confidence in your ability to do it too.

Let's say there's a woman you often see at the gym who's about your age and size who never wears a shirt over her sports bra and doesn't have rock-hard abs—like 99 percent of us. Your gym is always downright hot, but you cover up on top because it's just what you do. *I could never show my stomach, but jeez she looks so comfortable in her own skin. I bet it would feel great to ditch this damn T-shirt.* At first, you might even be critical—why would she show so much midriff? But your criticism (which is often envy in disguise) starts to morph into admiration. After you spot her a few more times (and she gives you a friendly nod), you begin to admire her ability to boldly lunge and squat without a sign of self-consciousness and think, *If she can do it, so can I.* You ditch that T-shirt and never look back. *This feels great! What was I waiting for?*

Model the friend who sends back their entrée when it arrives lukewarm instead of hot and send back your next disappointing meal. Follow the lead of the newly divorced friend who watches YouTube videos to learn how to do the home repairs their ex always took care of and finally fix that leaky pipe yourself. Or observe the parent at your kid's school who is always the first to question when something doesn't sit right with them and gets issues resolved. Dare to raise your hand at the next school board meeting.

Depending on the situation, there can be a fine line between being bold and being brassy or a jerk. I'm not recommending you model bad behavior. I'm suggesting you notice how the bold people around you get what they want in a way you haven't yet tried—or dared to try. After all, if *they* can do it, you can too. Right? Right.

BOLD MOVE

Make it a habit to observe the bold people around you successfully tackle and complete tasks. The more you see how they do it, the more skills you'll be able to add to your bundle of bold (more on that later).

Find a Bold Whisperer

Angie Cella, a single mom of four, woke up one morning after having had a dream to create a fun children's toy—specifically, a simple crafting tool for kids to add decorative, sparkly faux gems to their hair, clothing, and accessories. Cella was determined to make what she'd later call Blinger come to life.

After raising $10,000 from friends and family through Kickstarter, Cella still needed additional funds to make her literal dream come true. She also needed the support of her four children, and she credits them for believing in her through all the ups and downs. At one point, Cella asked her children what they thought about the idea of her selling their home and moving into an apartment, at least temporarily, so she'd have the funds to keep going with Blinger. Cella's eldest child said, "You've got to do it, Mom." And so she sold the house, along with half of their belongings, and had enough funds for several rounds of engineers and to get her invention in front of the toy industry.

In 2018, Cella registered for a booth at the annual Toy Fair Dallas, an industry event where the largest companies like Mattel and Hasbro, along with small emerging toy companies, exhibit their latest toys and games. She also participated in the "Women in Toys" event to boost the profile of Blinger.

Blinger (and Angie Cella!) was the star of the toy show. Several toy companies showed interest in licensing Blinger, including Wicked Cool Toys (now part of Jazwares), where Blinger found its home. In February 2019, Cella was on hand at the Wicked Cool Toys booth at the North American International Toy Fair in New York to present her invention to retailers and the press. Blinger went on to make many holiday gift lists and was nominated for "Creative Toy of the Year" in 2020.

Cella credits the encouragement she got from her kids, and her Christian faith, for her enormous success. Encouragement from the right sources goes a long way, especially when we have those inevitable moments of self-doubt. Ask a good friend, your partner, a family member, a mentor, or someone else you trust and respect to support your bold efforts. Even the kids in your life can be a strong positive influence.

BOLD MOVE

Asking for a little backup when you do something that is bolder than normal is a bold move in itself. Confide in one or two trusted people about your efforts, and explain why their support, even for small wins, helps you become bolder and get the life you want. Your handpicked cheerleading squad can help you conquer self-doubt and boost your ability to succeed.

Saying Is Believing

The phrase "saying is believing" is not just a popular axiom; it's a long-held social-psychology theory known as the saying-is-believing effect.

When we say something out loud to someone else, we tend to believe what we said. And when we are seeking advice or supportive tips before making a bold move, it might be just as effective, if not more, to give someone else that same advice.

A good friend, an influencer before they were called "influencers," called to ask me for my advice on a deal he'd been approached with, since I regularly negotiate deals on behalf of my clients. An emerging sports brand with a hot new product asked my friend, a respected athlete, to be their spokesperson. The offer was way below his normal fee, but he understood they didn't have the budget of the more established brands he'd partnered with in the past. Still, accepting the offer would be selling himself short and he knew it. Sort of. He was still grappling with his imposter syndrome—his belief that he wasn't as good as others thought he was. And I knew that was bothering him.

My friend had come to his great success because of talent and perseverance. "This whole famous thing," as he refers to it, came as a complete shock. He wasn't sure he was deserving of all the adulation he'd been receiving. A young fan told him he was the reason he'd decided to buckle down in high school, adding that he'd ended up with a college scholarship to compete in his sport. A young woman told him he'd inspired her to run her first marathon after losing her husband, an avid marathoner, to cancer.

My friend didn't want to pass on the deal, but he also didn't want to risk overreaching and losing the offer by asking for more money. He knew that this deal would likely lead to more young people discovering him and becoming inspired to take bold moves themselves.

It was a weird time to be asking for my advice. I was quietly dealing with my own version of imposter syndrome. I'd been approached by a friend, a big donor active with a major nonprofit based in Los Angeles, who said the organization was looking for "A-list speakers to inspire guests" at their upcoming annual event, and that he'd recommended me. He said I should follow up with them for consideration and shared the contact information. I thanked my friend profusely, as the chance to get in front of these notable Angelenos was a great business opportunity for me. I told him I was interested but would have to check my calendar, making something up about my pending travel schedule.

Here's the truth: I had no conflict with the date, but I did have self-doubt. I thought gathering and submitting all the information the committee needed to make their decision would be a waste of time. "A-list speaker to inspire guests." *Me?* I didn't think I stood a chance. These people were well-connected. Surely there would be a dozen high-profile speakers on the list they'd choose over me.

It was not long after that negative self-talk that my friend called asking for advice on his deal. Without hesitation, I switched into Bold Gear and told my pal what I thought. I reminded him why he is worth what he knows he is worth, and that if he undervalued himself, he couldn't expect the brand to value his worth either, once the deal was sealed. Then I said: "I believe in you, and I believe that you deserve this opportunity. You have the ability to inspire so many people and the brand will be very proud to have you as their spokesperson. Remember, they approached *you*! They want *you*! You've got this—go and get it!"

It was just the boost of confidence he needed. And it felt great to be the one to give it to him. My friend went back to the brand with a number and they upped their offer to something close to it. He accepted the terms with no regret.

After hanging up the phone, I realized I'd just told my friend exactly what *I* needed to hear. *I am worthy of this opportunity to speak at the donor event. After all, they approached* me*! They want* me*!*

I immediately texted my donor friend and said, "I'm in!" and sent over what the committee needed to make their decision. Giving advice to my friend not only made me feel pretty good, but it also boosted my confidence. Plus, it would be pretty hypocritical of me not to take my own advice. Here's the epilogue: I didn't get picked for the big-time speaking gig, but I was glad I tossed my hat in the ring. Rejection is much easier to recover from than regret—something we'll discuss later. I would have kicked myself had I not tried, and by putting myself out there as a candidate, I signaled to my friend (and, importantly, to myself!)

that I was open to future speaking opportunities, which eventually came my way.

BOLD MOVE

When someone you know needs that saying-is-believing boost, give it to them. It might just be exactly what *you* need to hear to make your next bold move.

Appoint Your Bold of Directors

My friend approached me for advice on his deal because he trusted my professional instincts—negotiating fees is what I do for my clients. But most of us don't have expert advisors on call, so we naturally seek input from our partner, family, friends, and coworkers.

Of course, you can turn to the experts when you need to. Need legal advice? Ask an attorney. Need spiritual advice? Ask your priest, rabbi, imam, or shaman. Need help figuring out what that rash is? Ask your doctor. But when it comes to asking for advice on making your next bold move? Ask your Bold of Directors.

Find others who are also looking to build their bold and invite them to form an informal group to advise and support each other. (You may already have the makings of such a group within your circle of friends.) Not only will you all receive helpful, encouraging messages when you need them, but you'll reap the benefits of giving advice, support, and encouragement. It's a win-win. No matter which side of the equation you're on—problem-haver or problem-solver— you will be boosting your own confidence and self-efficacy.

Not the type to ask for help? The most successful people I know are the ones most able to admit their weaknesses and ask for the help they need to get to the next step. Put your pride aside and seek out the best guidance you can find. I surround myself with people who are much more capable at the things I am bad at. These are people I trust to ask for advice, help, and support.

BOLD MOVE

Bold, successful people know that success never happens in a vacuum. It takes a village, but not just any village. Choose your Bold of Directors wisely. Surround yourself with people who want the best for you and want to see you succeed, and you them. If you're looking for an instant Bold of Directors and are open to meeting new people, consider joining an established mastermind group or starting your own. You can find groups online.

Holy Bold, Batman!

This tip is inspired by my kids. When they were little, they liked to role-play and dress up like their favorite superheroes or the latest movie or cartoon characters they were obsessed with. I was always amazed at their immediate transformation into those characters. To be fair, my son and daughter have always been confident kids, but add a Batman cape or Wonder Woman gold cuffs and they both immediately morphed into children with greater strength, power, and courage.

Turns out, my kids (and probably many of the kids in your life) were onto something. In 2016, researchers Rachel White and Emily Prager (along with others, including *Grit* author Angela Duckworth) studied four-to-six-year-olds to gauge their level of focus and perseverance at a work task when they responded to questions as themselves, in third person, and when they imagined themselves to be Batman or another favorite character. When the children were self-distancing—meaning they had separated their real identity and leaned into their alter ego—their concentration on the task and their resolve and perseverance to complete the task successfully increased. The researchers dubbed this the "Batman effect."

Having an alter ego doesn't just serve young children. Researchers report that self-distancing enables adults to leave feelings of insecurity and anxiety behind, while boosting our feelings of control and confidence with the task at hand. In other words, self-distancing by using an alter ego enhances our self-efficacy.

Even major stars have seen the benefits of an alter ego. Beyoncé has said Sasha Fierce, her self-created alter ego, "boosts her confidence and improves her performance."

Former Spice Girl Victoria Beckham says her Posh Spice persona "fast-tracked" her to finding her "inner confidence and self-belief." And then there's the story of the golden-age Hollywood actor who wanted to escape his modest and troubled upbringing. Archibald Alec Leach became Cary Grant, his glamorous alter ego who lived the life of the handsome, debonair actor we remember. Todd Herman, author of *The Alter Ego Effect*, refers to the power of the alter ego with this quote from the late actor: "I pretended to be somebody I wanted to be and I finally became that person. Or he became me. Or we met at some point." Herman says that when you are truly acting, behaving, and thinking like your alter ego, you eventually absorb what you need to and can become a better, more effective version of yourself.

BOLD MOVE

Try an alter ego on for size and put it into action the next time you need a boost of confidence. That could even mean digging into your closet for your own version of a superhero cape or set of gold wrist cuffs. For the last five years, I've worn a Wonder Woman pendant around my neck—a gift from a dear (bold!) friend and a little reminder to act like a can-do, kick-ass person every day. She took it off her own neck and put it on mine when I needed a bold boost, and I've given the same necklace to dozens of friends. It's my way of spreading the Batman effect!

Listen to Yourself (Your Other Self)

When the organizer for TEDxBuckhead invited me to give a talk, I felt fortunate, honored, and scared out of my mind.

I'm very insecure about public speaking. I can meet someone for the first time and within minutes ask them personal questions about their life and work without flinching. I can host a celebrity or brilliant scientist on my *Habits & Hustle* podcast and talk to them for hours without a moment of shyness. But put me onstage in front of an audience—whether it's 20 people or 1,020—and I freeze up with insecurity and self-doubt. Just thinking about giving a TEDx talk made me incredibly anxious, and I turned down the offer.

My negative self-talk went something like this:

Who do you think you are, thinking you can give a TEDx talk? You get so nervous about speaking in public! You'll mess up! And do you really think you have something that important or relevant or interesting to say to these people?

And then, I stopped myself. I let another voice chime in:

Of course you have something important, relevant, and interesting to say! That's why they called you. Your fear of failure is holding you back from getting what you want. You got this!

To pivot from "no way" to "sign me up," I called on the boldness tool I use when I want to drive up my confidence and drive out my negative self-talk. It's a combination of saying-is-believing and the Batman effect, and it gives me a double dose of self-efficacy.

Ethan Kross, PhD, author of *Chatter: The Voice in Our Head, Why It Matters, and How to Harness It* (and a researcher on the Batman effect), says that when our inner voice is blathering on with self-doubt or ruminating over the potential (disastrous) consequences of our next bold move, we have the opportunity to reverse course and put our chatter to productive use.

Kross suggests trying "distanced self-talk." We give our inner chatterbox its own type of alter ego—one that champions our abilities just like a coach or good friend would. Then, we let the chatter give us the advice and encouragement we need. In my case, it went something like this:

> *Jen, you can do this. You can do this! This could be the most important, life-changing talk you have ever given! And what's the worst that can happen? If even just one person gets your message and gets over their fear of failure and makes bold moves to chase what they want, that's enough! You've done your job. And there's no one better to give this advice than you!*

And that was it. My inner chatterbox/alter ego gave me its best advice, and it worked. I called the organizer back and said, "I'll do it!" And I did!

Did that mean my TEDx talk was a breeze? No. I was the most nervous I've ever been. In fact, you can probably see my anxiety in action if you watch my talk: www.youtube.com /watch?v=wM82hE6oimw. At one point, my mouth was so dry from nerves that I had to ask them to stop recording so I could get a glass of water. Speakers aren't allowed notes onstage, and I was so scared I'd forget something important that, if you look closely, you'll see notes written on my hand. But even with my cheat sheet I still forgot two minutes of my speech!

It was one of the hardest talks I've ever done because of what it represented. Was I perfectly polished? No. Did I fumble here and there? Yes. But I got through it, in part thanks to listening to my bold inner voice coaching me along the way, reminding me to take my own damn advice to overcome my fears and keep going: *Jennifer! Your message is strong and true! There's no reason to be scared! And even if you are, that's OK! But that's not a reason to stop!*

When it was over, when the audience applauded and wanted to know more, when the YouTube views passed one million, then two, three, four, and counting, I was so glad I listened to that voice in my head—the bold voice, that is.

BOLD MOVE

Next time your fear and self-doubt are stopping you from making a bold move, listen to your self-talk carefully. Slip an alter ego over your inner chatterbox and see what happens. Here's a practical way to do that if you have a voice memo function on your cell phone. Record yourself as you let your negative self-talk rip. Just let it all out. Don't hold back. Then go back and listen, but with your bold alter ego ready to "talk back." As you play back your voice memo, pause from time to time and answer your fears with boldness. And once again, don't hold back! It's an eye-opening (ear-opening) experience.

The George Costanza Effect

One of my favorite *Seinfeld* episodes of all time is called "The Opposite," where George Costanza stumbles upon the power of doing things, yes, "the opposite." George, in his own words, is a bald man with no job and no money who lives with his parents. "My life," he laments, "is the complete opposite of what I want it to be." Seized by the urge to ditch his loser lifestyle (and egged on by Jerry), he embraces his "opposite philosophy" and begins acting in a way that's a total 180 compared to his usual behavior. By the end of the episode, George lands a beautiful girlfriend, a new apartment, and a job with the New York Yankees. How the hell did George Costanza get a job with the *Yankees*? He did "the opposite" of what he would normally have done in the interview. Instead of bending over backward to show his admiration for owner George Steinbrenner, George ripped him to pieces. It worked! Steinbrenner loved it! And George got the job.

I'm not suggesting you rip into your potential employer in a job interview, or anyone else for that matter. But I *do* recommend you play with what's been dubbed the "George Costanza effect," inspired by this *Seinfeld* episode, and do things the opposite of how you normally would. It may take a bit of channeling your alter ego, but it can get results! Not the kind of person who'd ever approach the cute girl at the bar? Be that person. Never the one to get up and sing at the karaoke bar? Grab that songbook! Not a dog person? Offer to take your friend's pooch to the local dog park (you should probably like dogs at least a little for that one). Does your desk always look like a hurricane blew through? Take a half hour and clear it off.

Shifting your behavior from what's expected can yield unexpected (and positive) results. Studies show that breaking old routines and exploring different ways of doing things, even by doing them the opposite way of how you normally do them, challenges your brain to form new pathways. And when you explore new ways of doing things and find success at that, you're building your self-efficacy.

You may find that some of your new habits stick—you could have a new partner, a furry pet, and a clean desk—or you may still hate karaoke! But the point is, you're pushing yourself, and that's part of flexing your bold muscles.

BOLD MOVE

Do you always roll your eyes at the latest TikTok dance craze? Embrace "the opposite" and learn it, do it, post it! Share it with me @therealjencohen.

Principle #4

Change Your Mind

GROWING UP IN THE '70S and '80s, I was part of the latch-key generation, as were many other kids from working-parent families. I became very self-reliant and was able to manage for myself when I walked into an empty house after school.

Because my mom worked full-time, I got home before her every day and was on my own. I was expected to do my homework and chores before turning on the TV to watch *Three's Company*. If I had trouble with my assignments, I'd call one of my classmates for help or leave a note for my mom and walk over to my friend's house with my schoolbag on my back, no matter how dark and cold those Winnipeg winter evenings were.

It's possible that my boldness took root out of necessity, but there's no question that my bold mindset grew stronger every time I opened the door to that empty house and did things for myself. Though I had two loving parents who supported me completely, I was also tuned in to working for what I needed. I had many opportunities to show my parents that I was responsible and could take care of myself, and as a result I developed the freedom to chase what I wanted from a young age.

Be Antifragile:
A Lesson from the Boldest Generation

My Generation X upbringing fueled my budding boldness and tenaciousness, and my friends were the same way. Gen Xers walked, biked, or took public transportation by ourselves or with other young people, no parents required. We made our own plans to hang out with friends or go to the mall—and made our own "mall money" to spend there.

It wasn't that our parents didn't care about us. They just didn't find it necessary to watch over our every move. Time alone meant we got to know ourselves as individuals. We became skilled at taking care of ourselves and honed our independence. We became adaptable to problems and situations as they arose and found solutions as best we could. Our self-efficacy and confidence grew. We were comfortable taking calculated risks and reaped the rewards, dealt with the blows, and built up our resilience. If we failed, we recovered and went right back to pushing the limits.

It's a lesson in boldness to look at what some kids born between 1964 and 1981 have done with their lives. Of course, there have been game-changing thinkers and doers before and since Gen X, but my generation has become notable for our creativity and individualism.

We can boast mavericks in many fields, including innovators and entrepreneurs like Elon Musk (Tesla, SpaceX); Sara Blakely (Spanx); Larry Page and Sergey Brin (Google); Jawed Karim, Steve Chen, and Chad Hurley (YouTube); Sheryl Sandberg (Meta, LeanIn.org); Jack Dorsey (Twitter, Square); Jimmy Wales and Larry Sanger (Wikipedia); Jeff Bezos (Amazon, Blue Origin); and many more. We have groundbreaking writers like Brené Brown and J. K. Rowling; a wonderful diversity of artists and entertainers like Lin-Manuel Miranda, Jennifer Lopez, and Mary J. Blige; and sports figures who shattered barriers and broke records like Tiger Woods, Tom Brady, and the Williams sisters.

Many people who've studied Gen Xers think our generation was especially primed for big things because we grew up with so much independence. We were left to our own devices to figure stuff out (and if we blew it, we had to figure it out again). That persistence and fortitude, some say, is why we have been so successful at launching products and services that solve problems. Because of our individualism and I-can-do-it-myself attitude, we rarely needed others to get us where we wanted to be. We didn't have to ask permission to take small risks. And those habits stayed with us as adults, when we leapt into problem-solving and got things done. Of course we've had our failures. I sure have, and every name on that lineup above had more than one! We got hurt. We bombed. We fell down, hard. But we got ourselves right back up again. We learned from our mistakes. We are what essayist and onetime options trader and risk analyst Nassim Nicholas Taleb calls "antifragile."

To be antifragile, Taleb says, is to "benefit from shocks; [to] thrive and grow when exposed to volatility, randomness, disorder, and stressors and love adventure, risk, and uncertainty." Taleb argues that "antifragility is beyond resilience or robustness." We get better from the "shocks" we experience, not simply more resilient to them.

Today's generation of kids and young adults are less able to reap the positive benefits of antifragility, since many were raised during the age of helicopter parenting in a culture of "safetyism" (a term popularized by Greg Lukianoff and Jonathan Haidt in *The Coddling of the American Mind: How Good Intentions and Bad Ideas Are Setting Up a Generation for Failure*). In a world where everyone gets a trophy so they never feel disappointed in their own failures, and where trigger warnings and microaggressions mean never having to feel hurt or offended, and where every moment of free time seems to be scheduled with structured activity, risks aren't taken. No bones are broken. The kids, who eventually grow into adults, remain fragile.

But you simply cannot be bold and get what you want if you don't build up your ability to survive the challenges of life when things don't go your way, when success doesn't come easy, when you cannot anticipate the benefits of taking a risk and are too fearful to even try.

When you prioritize protecting yourself from any damage or insult to your mind, body, and emotions, you can't grow. You've wrapped yourself up in a protective shell but your safety nets are more like spiderwebs and you're trapped. You're OK with good enough, even inadequate, because you're safe from hurt and fear. You accept a lesser life.

You've probably heard the term "self-acceptance" in discussions about accepting your limits or accepting things the way they are. Depending on what's going on in your life, particularly if there's a powerful external force you can't control, sometimes that can be a healthy attitude. *Hey, it is what it is, and I just have to get through this.* But . . . sometimes we're tempted to take that concept too far, particularly when what we want seems so out of our reach. *It is what it is, and it will never be anything better.* Self-acceptance becomes an excuse to never try, to give up going after what you want because of your weaknesses and challenges.

To me, self-acceptance means you accept your weaknesses and challenges not as setbacks but as drivers to move you forward. It means using them to try even harder to go after bigger, better things. In my world, mediocrity, weaknesses, and challenges are not an excuse to remain where you are. In my world, you don't give yourself permission to be a loser. And you certainly don't get a trophy for that. In the bigger, better, bolder world, nothing deters you from going after what you want.

Gen Xers may have gotten a head start on their journey to being bold, but it doesn't really matter when you were born. It's never too late to become self-aware. Get to know your weaknesses, your triggers, the things that hurt you, disappoint you, and frustrate you. Push against them. Don't hide from them. And do not let them control your destiny. The higher your self-awareness, the higher your chance of success; self-awareness leads to self-acceptance, which leads to boldness.

Does Your Mindset Need a Reset?

Fear is a bold killer, but the fact is we all have fears—of rejection, of failure, of shame. I have faced my own self-doubt, the root of fear, as far back as I can remember. I was awkward and clumsy, and you already know I wasn't a brainiac. But you also know that I learned early on to embrace my weaknesses and use them as strengths, a practice that changed my perspective on life and what I could take from it.

It takes time. You can't just wake up after a nap and transform your personality from fearful to bold. But you can start the process right now. Use the ideas below to give yourself a "brain transplant"—a bold brain transplant.

Big Bold Reset: Tell Fear to Get Out of Your Way

Belief in yourself is the bedrock of boldness. Once you can build on that belief, you naturally begin to shed the self-doubt, limited thinking, fear, and excuses that are holding you back.

Ask yourself this: Where would you be a year from today if you didn't have any fear? Where would you be five years from now if you didn't let your limiting beliefs hold you back? The only way to move forward is to let go of the fear, but you must take action to make that happen; such action is the opposite of the making-excuses brand of self-acceptance described above.

I'm not saying it's easy, or that it's the same process for everyone, but I do know that bold actions, however small at first, are the ultimate antidote to self-doubt and its partner, fear of failure. And the alternative—staying stuck—is ultimately more harmful than whatever you're afraid of.

Dr. Suma Chand, a clinical cognitive behavioral psychologist, says that fear and anxiety trap us so that we cannot move forward. It's an awful, paralyzing feeling. "The more you feed it, the stronger it grows," Dr. Chand says of fear. "After a while, you're avoiding the discomfort of the fear itself, rather than the thing you fear. When you avoid the things you fear, you feel safe and comfortable, and you don't want to do anything that will shake this safe cocoon of comfort." For this sense of safety, "you pay a heavy price—your freedom to live your life the way you really want to live," Dr. Chand says.

There is a solution. Researchers have found that systematic exposure to what we fear is the best way to get over those fears. In other words, instead of letting fears imprison you, expose yourself to them. Stand right up to that fear. Or sit down next to it. Or call it on the phone. I don't care how you face your fear, just face it. Face it hard. And it will give way.

Start with one small step. A little fear. Get rid of a teeny tiny little spider. Try on a teeny tiny polka-dot bikini. Request a small favor from someone you've been afraid to approach. Build up your immunity to your fears bit by bit, increasing the size of the fear each time. Gradually, your confidence will strengthen and grow with each fear you expose yourself to. Step-by-step, you'll become bolder.

I admit that I still go out of my way to avoid my fears, like public speaking. I get intimidated by the big stuff, where a lot is on the line—as all of us do. But by exposing myself to my fears, I get stronger at facing them down and neutralizing them. I don't want to make a fool out of myself when I speak in front of insanely intelligent MIT students and faculty, or fumble when I'm interviewing guests on my podcast (especially because I'm generally in awe of their brilliance), because I worry that I'll blow it.

Yet, these days I worry less and less, because I face that fear head-on, over and over again. My podcast requires me to interview people nearly every day, and it has gotten so natural and feels so easy that there's no significant fear factor. As for public speaking, I just know that I have to practice—a lot! And so I do. What I don't do is give up. And with every victory, I'm emboldened by the thrill of getting past what's holding me back and getting what I want on the other side. A great podcast episode or an engaged audience that asks questions means that my message is getting out there, which is precisely what I want!

Big Bold Reset: Dump Your Self-Doubts

What do you fear? What do you dodge in order to feel safe? Do you avoid asking for a raise you believe you deserve because if the answer is no, you'll feel rejected and of lesser value to the company? Do you avoid telling a friend she is mistreating you for fear you'll lose that friend? Do you avoid asking for help because someone will think you're weak? Do you avoid going to the gym because you feel people will judge the way you look? What do you avoid that would otherwise make your life better if you didn't?

Our quality of life is deeply affected by avoiding actions that make us uncomfortable, even if taking those actions would make our lives better. At some point, we no longer can see what we are missing out on. I'm not saying you should jump out of a plane in order to overcome your fear of heights and to see what you're missing by not getting an aerial view of the city. I'm talking about smaller, everyday actions that you go out of your way to sidestep. It's those little everyday fears tapping us on the shoulder that can do the most damage, not the fear of getting caught between a grizzly bear mama and her cubs. *Don't take on that project because you'll be in over your head . . . don't wear that because you're too old . . . don't plan that trip because you've never been there . . . don't ask her for that because she'll say no . . .*

Fear is not your friend. It's not there to keep you safe, even though that's what we often think. (Granted, sometimes that's the case—always avoid coming between a bear and her cubs.) Everyday fears—of rejection, failure, shame, and inadequacy—exist to keep you from a bigger, better, bolder life. And they have a common root cause: self-doubt.

Self-doubt is why we get stuck in a shitty job or never make the money we deserve. *I don't think I have what it takes to get ahead.*

Self-doubt is why we get stuck in a relationship we don't want to be in or have no relationships at all. *No one else would ever want to be with me.*

Self-doubt is why we give up on our physical well-being. *I'm not strong enough to stick with a fitness plan and I don't know how to eat healthy.*

Self-doubt is why we don't go public with our creative efforts. *I will never be able to make a living as an actor/painter/writer/musician . . . so many others are better than I am.*

Self-doubt is the reason why we never take action to chase what we want, whether it's career goals, relationships, self-care, creative passions, or any other number of areas. And it seems like it plays on repeat every time we have the opportunity to take action. What's on your self-doubt tape? What's keeping you from making a change and moving toward the rich life you want? Use the skills you've learned in Principle #3—You Gotta Believe—to kick your self-doubt to the curb, and stay tuned for more tips as you work through the rest of the Principles.

Big Bold Reset: Toss the Baggage, Keep the Luggage

My friend Tamar has one of the biggest, best, boldest attitudes about life I've ever encountered. She has been fighting cancer for a while now, working full-time while she goes through treatment. A few years ago, amid all this, her daughter Kaila was also diagnosed with a different form of cancer. Tamar lives in Los Angeles and her daughter lived in New York, but every other week, after her chemo, Tamar got on a plane and flew east to be with Kaila and help care for her. Regular cross-country flights are tiring enough when you're totally healthy, but Tamar wanted to be with her daughter and nothing, including cancer, was going to stop her. She chased what she wanted—precious time with her daughter—and she got it.

When I called Tamar after being out of touch for a bit and she told me Kaila had finally lost her battle, I was stunned. How, I asked her, could she just answer the phone and talk to me and not be . . . shattered?

"Why would I not answer the phone?" she said. "There is possibility in everything," including a conversation with a friend. And that idea—that there is possibility, even in the darkest of times, and that life is made up of opportunities—sums up Tamar's approach to living with boldness. Tamar grieves for her daughter, but, as she says, while real life "is messy and dirty and sad, it's also the good stuff. You can focus on the good or you can focus on the shit. I choose to focus on the good." And so she perseveres.

When she goes to chemo, she dresses in style and puts on her hot-pink coat. She doesn't think, "Ugh, crap, I'm going to chemo . . . " It's more like, "I'm going to chemo and I'm going to walk in looking like I own the place!" (Here's the Batman effect in action. If putting on your own version of a hot-pink coat helps you feel more confident and hopeful, do it.)

There's a fine line, Tamar says, between being in a rut and being in a groove. She faces the uncertainty of her illness and grief over Kaila's death every day, but rather than feeling like she's fallen into a rut (and waste energy blaming someone or something), she chooses to live life in the groove—taking action to change her situation as much as she can. She can't reverse her daughter's fate or her own diagnosis, but she can keep moving forward.

When you don't do anything, when you just sit there and accept what has been handed to you, when you point fingers and make excuses, that's when you get trapped in a rut, Tamar says. Taking action—even if it's just a baby step toward getting what you want—has the opposite effect, the antidote to life in a rut. And taking action, especially in the face of obstacles, is also shorthand for being bold.

What Are You Carrying Around?

"I'm not so strong," Tamar says, when I applaud her strength and fearlessness. "I'm just choosing not to have baggage." Baggage is hanging on to regrets and toxic relationships or situations; it's ruminating over what's gone wrong in your life and what will go wrong in the future. Instead, Tamar suggests we bring something else on our journey.

"When you're feeling fearless about life, you're carrying 'luggage,'" she says. Luggage is what you carry when you're flying off to an adventure—just what you need and nothing more. Luggage is light and filled with possibilities. Baggage holds you back, has no purpose, and gets in your way. You don't pack a winter coat when you go on a beach vacation. What purpose would it serve? Why go through life with heavy things that only serve to weigh you down and slow your journey, especially if that burden just gets heavier with time? Leave all that baggage behind.

Your old boss who treated you terribly? Leave him behind when you start your next job. The old girlfriend who crushed your heart? Leave her behind as you begin dating again. Lose money in the stock market? Leave that behind and invest in your future. *Live.*

"I'm grateful to have the ability to live life despite having cancer. Every day, I choose to travel lightly and live fearlessly," Tamar says.

What are you dragging around in your baggage? Open up that suitcase and dump what's holding you back, especially the things—the people, the experiences, the self-doubt, and the fear—that are weighing you down.

BAGGAGE VS. LUGGAGE

Baggage	Luggage
Negative	Positive
Bringing the past with you	Going somewhere
Living in the past	Learning from the past
Holding you back	Pushing you forward
Basic	Luxurious
Necessary	Important

Big Bold Reset: Change Your Environment, Change Your Brain

Imagine you're driving your car home from work, taking the same route you always take. You have a lot on your mind. You're upset with the way your new boss spoke to you a few hours earlier. They were condescending and dismissive of your ideas, reminding you of how your father talked to you when you were a little kid. Your new boss has a different way of doing business and doesn't want to listen to you or your opinion, even though you've been with the company for nearly a decade and know a thing or two. It's as if all your hard work and dedication to the company was erased the minute the new boss came on board. Maybe you'll say something the next time they brush you off. Or maybe you'll just spend time building a boss's trust all over again, just like you did a few years ago with that other bozo. It's all so incredibly frustrating and . . .

. . . you pull into your driveway. *How the hell did I get here?*

While your thoughts distracted you from focusing on the drive home, you still managed to find your way there, safe and sound, as if you went on autopilot. There you are, sitting in your car in your driveway, grateful to your unconscious mind for taking the wheel.

Everyday actions, regular habits, and daily rituals generally don't require our conscious mind. I don't overthink how to brush my teeth, for example. I just go through the motions and generally think about something else. I don't concentrate on how to walk, I just walk. I don't think about how to ride my bike, I just ride the bike. When something becomes second nature, we don't need to tap into our consciousness or think too hard about what we're doing.

The unconscious mind partners with the conscious mind so that the conscious mind can focus on new tasks. For example, I'm not consciously thinking about where each key is located on my laptop keyboard as I type this sentence. My conscious mind is focused on what to write—the harder task that requires more of my brain—not how to type. And what I'm typing is likely something I mulled over while I was driving or walking or washing my hair. In fact, much of my creative thinking happens while I'm doing something on autopilot, when my mind is free to wander. (Don't worry—I'm paying attention to the road!)

Unfortunately, our unconscious mind also goes on autopilot in ways that can block a bold mindset. You may be driving along that same route home and you pass, as always, your old middle school, which you rarely think about. But today you're in such a funk from work that just the sight of it reminds you of how you felt inadequate—not smart enough, few friends, mean teachers. Or, you walk into a clothing store to grab a few T-shirts and see the swimsuits, which triggers a whole slew of negative thoughts about your body. A friend's birthday dinner sets off a loop of *I'm a loser*, thinking about another year of your life going by, with so many of your goals still out of reach. Just when your brain is humming along on autopilot, you encounter something in your environment that causes a cascade of negative thinking.

As the cognitive therapist Dr. Jeffrey Nevid puts it, "Negative thoughts impose harsh judgments on our abilities, harp on our character flaws, portend terrible consequences that lay ahead, instigate anger and prompt aggressive responses, and nag us about our weaknesses, mistakes, and misgivings. When they prick us, we experience corresponding emotions of fear, anger, guilt, worry, and so on. They also dampen our self-worth or how we think of ourselves."

It's just a big cycle that seems unbreakable, but you *can* break it. Start with this small action step suggested by Dr. Nevid: He recommends we consciously make a note of our triggers by asking ourselves the following questions and journaling our responses. This practice can help us become aware of what triggers our negative self-talk and begin to try and override it with positive thoughts.

- *What thoughts are going through my mind?*

- *What am I thinking about?*

- *What memories does this feeling evoke?*

- *What am I saying to myself under my breath?*

I'm not a believer in running away from challenges, but I do believe there is an easy way to remove the triggers that stop you from being bold: Change your environment. I don't mean move across the country or redecorate your living room. Instead, look around, consider your daily routine, and inventory your everyday triggers, little things that cause big (bad) thinking. Hate the feeling of inadequacy you get when you drive by your old middle school? Take a new way to work for a while. Does that shirt in the closet remind you of your ex? Put it in the giveaway bag and get it out of the house. Trying to cut back on the chips? Then don't keep bags of them in the kitchen.

Recently I had a birthday and ate half (OK, three-fourths) of the cake myself—it was right in front of me and my "bad" autopilot picked that fork up and went for it! I confess I have a weakness for cake (especially ice-cream cake). And I love a good all-you-can-eat buffet (especially if there is cake involved). I may be a fitness expert, but I still love food, and left to my own devices will overindulge. To stop that from happening, I make an effort to avoid having temptations (like cake) in my personal space. Environment trumps willpower. So I change my environment.

Put an ice-cream cake in front of me and I'll have a slice, or two, or three. Put video games in front of me, and I have zero interest. Meanwhile, a friend who never touches sugary carbs will stay up all night playing video games, even when he has promised himself to only play "one quick game" before bed. (If he'd move the console out of the bedroom, I have a feeling he'd be able to keep his promise!)

Think of all the ways your everyday environment distracts you from moving forward with your goals. Let's take the big one first: personal tech. How many times a day do you check social media? Email? Have you ever taken precious time to respond to a post from a total stranger just because you couldn't resist? How often are you interrupted by a ping on your phone? How many tabs do you have open on your laptop, only a couple of which are relevant to what is really important? How many posts by friends or random people in your feed about the latest news controversy do you read and get worked up about? How much news do you consume because you "have to stay informed," only to realize you just learned nothing as you wasted a half hour watching the politicians and pundits talking over each other?

Be the master of what you let into your conscious and unconscious mind. Temptations and triggers can derail our belief in ourselves. Don't make it hard for yourself to keep on track. The best way to design a bold-boosting environment is to fill it up with easy ways to focus and be positive. Want to read a chapter of a book each day? Leave the printed book near your favorite spot on the couch, open to the next chapter. Want to go for a run in the mornings? Leave out your running shoes, socks, shorts, and top. Want to quit buying candy bars and salty snacks? Don't go shopping when you're starving.

Creating a bigger, better, bolder life is about collecting the people, places, and experiences that enrich your life. That rarely includes an idiotic Instagram post from a C-list celebrity influencer who will be yesterday's news this time tomorrow. Make room to collect what you want in life by cutting out the things that trip you up. Your bold move today could be as simple as turning your phone off while you journal about your fears and triggers, or putting it on "focus" mode during the rest of the day so that you're not sidetracked by a million pings.

Just as it's important to eliminate distractions from your environment, make sure you include some bold influences, and that includes people. Get rid of the detractors and distractors and lean on your Bold of Directors! Surround yourself with friends and family who support your bold goals and strengthen your bold practices. A bold new environment means a bold new mindset.

Now that you're getting into the groove with a bold mindset, you can go bigger and better with a daily boldness workout, customized just for you. Read on for some habits and practices that will stretch and strengthen your bold muscles, so that you can chase the rich life you deserve.

Principle #5

Practice Bold Habits

BEFORE YOU BEGIN TO TAKE bigger, better, bolder actions, master the small things—including daily rituals that will fine-tune your direction toward a rich life.

We all have daily routines we barely even think about. We wake up, shower, dress, and maybe brew some coffee before we head to work. If we have kids, that's a whole routine in itself. We walk the dog and take out the recycling. We text our partner before we head home. We do the same things over and over again the same way. These are all productive practices, as mundane as some may seem. Remember, there is an upside to your brain going on autopilot. Overthinking and distractions sap your energy and slow down your bold moves.

If you're like me, you have little rituals already in place. If you don't you should, because having a routine makes life a lot easier. And be aware of the less-productive, mindless habits many of us practice—like reaching for our phones first thing and checking social media, or getting sidetracked by the latest non-news story before we get out of bed.

Even if you think of yourself as disciplined, nearly all of us can use a tune-up when it comes to our day-to-day habits. Check yourself to make sure you're not wasting time and energy. Instead, refine your daily routine to help you chase the life you want.

In the same way you can get rid of distracting thoughts that lead you into a cycle of negative thinking, you can rid yourself of habits that are unproductive and get in the way of living a bold life. When you change your usual way of doing things, you start the process of reprogramming your brain— the basis of neuroplasticity. You are actually "growing" your brain's neural pathways by doing things differently, essentially giving your bold brain muscles a workout!

If you do one or more of these already, add another one or try a new way of doing the rituals you currently practice, like exercising outside in nature instead of always going to a gym. I've included many of the daily rituals that work for me, but I know everyone is different. For example, I'm a true believer in meditation . . . for other people. It's just not for me—at least, not yet. I don't enjoy it, in part because I still can't get the hang of it (though I haven't given up). The point is this: you'll stick to your good habits if you choose the ones that you enjoy and that you can easily incorporate into your day.

With that in mind, choose the practices below that you believe suit you best. If one doesn't work for you after several attempts, go down the list and try another on for size. No matter which habits and rituals you choose to embrace, when done consistently they'll change your brain and strengthen your bold muscles.

The only practice I insist you add, if you're not already doing it, is exercise. I can assure you that, within weeks, you will not only feel physically stronger, but you will also be mentally stronger. Regular exercise supports a disciplined mindset, goal setting, self-confidence, and self-assurance. I fell in love with fitness when I was a teenager because I felt so much stronger inside and out; exercise has played a big role in my ability to be bold.

I've used the word "rituals" here, but whatever you choose to call your everyday activities—habits, routines, practices— here are some particularly effective ones to consider adding to your life, especially those that you've never tried before. You certainly don't need to do all of them. (I don't!) But engaging in just one new ritual every day is a bold muscle move that will help you grow stronger, in mind, body, and spirit.

Bold Mind Rituals

Tell Yourself a Gratitude Story

Before you assume this practice is about writing daily lists of ten things you are grateful for, keep reading, because it's not. New research points to a much more effective kind of gratitude practice that changes mindsets for the better.

Gratitude is a "prosocial" behavior and mindset. Prosocial in this context refers to the circuits in our brain and body associated with "approach" behaviors and mindsets, which lead to positive interactions with others, ourselves, and the things that bring us joy. This is exactly the kind of mindset we need to make bold moves, as opposed to our defensive neural circuits, which are associated with "avoidance" tendencies that lead to our feeling defensive, fearful, or stuck—or, worse, to moving backward.

We all get it, saying "thank you" is important. But when it comes to changing our brain, it's not giving thanks that works best, it's *receiving* thanks. Recent studies have found that someone showing us gratitude is much more potent in its effects on our neural circuitry. And the good news is that it doesn't have to be you who receives the thank-you.

Andrew Huberman, professor of neurobiology at Stanford University School of Medicine and host of the *Huberman Lab Podcast*, says we can trigger our prosocial neural circuitry when we think of a time we were shown genuine gratitude or when we recall a story when someone *else* felt deep gratitude toward someone and it really moved us.

Imagine stories like when a close family member shares how their physical therapist literally got them back on their feet after breaking a hip. Or the story a coworker told you about the Good Samaritan who went to the trouble of tracking her down and returning her lost wallet with all her cash still inside it. It can even be a historical video you watched about a mother's gratitude to a soldier for saving her child's life during a war.

Choose the gratitude story that really resonates with you. Huberman emphasizes that it must be a story that is genuine and authentic for this practice to work. Jot down bullet-point notes on the story you like, Huberman suggests, including:

- The struggle

- The help that was given

- How it impacts you emotionally

Then, Huberman says, take just a few minutes—even one minute will do—to repeat the story three times a week to yourself (or to another person), and to "think into the richness of that experience of receiving gratitude." This gratitude story will become very familiar to you and, in turn, in fewer than six weeks the neural circuits in your brain and nervous system that respond to this story will change your physiology.

This short gratitude practice, which can be done just about anywhere, has "outsized effects" on changing our state of mind and body, Huberman says. Unlike a meditation practice, where it can be a while before neuroplasticity takes effect, the activation of our prosocial circuits is instantaneous.

Your brain begins to change in the moment. "You immediately drop into the kind of optimal state [where] gratitude, and the circuits associated with it, appear to be especially plastic . . . just by simply reminding yourself of this particular narrative," Huberman explains.

How does this "especially plastic" gratitude practice prime you for boldness? This prosocial practice will shift the "functional connectivity of emotion pathways" to enhance your feelings of motivation and pursuit, while rewiring your fear circuits. You become more likely to move forward and take bold leaps. And much like every habit and Principle in this book, the more you practice, the bolder you will become.

Bold Body Rituals

Everyday Workouts with Extraordinary Results

Years ago, I was a personal trainer on a CW network reality competition show called *Shedding for the Wedding*, made by the same producers as NBC's *The Biggest Loser*. In this show, overweight couples competed to lose the most combined weight to win their dream wedding. Our filming time with the contestants was relatively short, and the workouts that my co-trainer Nicky Holender and I designed for them were admittedly tough.

The first couple of episodes were especially brutal for the couples, most of whom were new to fitness. But it didn't take long before each one of the contestants noticed that they were transforming not only physically, but also mentally. They pushed themselves, and their partners, beyond what they had believed were their limits. Week after week, I watched as their confidence grew while their weight dropped. The physical changes were dramatic, but the positive psychological changes were even more remarkable.

Months after the show wrapped, a few of the contestants reached out to share that losing weight and getting in shape had not only made them feel more attractive, but had also given them the emotional strength and courage to chase the life they wanted and not settle for the life they had. A few quit their jobs to pursue the careers they really wanted. One broke up with her fiancé because she realized that, while they had both changed for the better, their relationship had also transformed, and they needed to find the right partners for the people they'd become. One woman simply said she felt she had transformed into the person she always wanted to be.

The fact that the contestants reported that their physical transformation was at the core of their positive mental change was no surprise to me. I've trained celebrities who on the outside seemed like they had everything going for them. But it was once they began to make fitness a daily routine that they felt bolder about asking for the acting roles they wanted or the music they wanted to make.

One of the key benefits of exercise is how it connects the mind and body. Getting fit isn't about six-pack abs; it's about changing the chemicals in your brain. Getting fit makes you want to pursue healthier habits and break from destructive routines. It decreases stress levels while increasing your ability to go after bigger goals.

When you begin your morning with a workout, it keeps you on track for the rest of the day. You're more alert and focused, and you have much more energy than if you didn't work out. (Note: Most people seem to like the convenience of a morning workout—that's the best time for me—but others may prefer afternoons or even after work. Just pick a time that you can stick to.) I laugh when people tell me they don't have the energy to work out, because exercising gives you energy! And not just for your body, but your mind too. It enables you to switch gears from *I can't* to *I can and I will*—an unbelievable change of perspective.

If you're starting your exercise plan from scratch, it doesn't matter if your first move is a walk around the block or a ten-minute yoga practice you find on YouTube. Just start moving. Within days of a regular fitness routine, you'll be training your body and brain to give you the confidence for that bigger, better, bolder life. Do you need to work out every day? I do if I want to be as on point and focused as possible. In my view, working out is also the best antidepressant on the market, without any lousy side effects. You may not need to do your regular workout seven days a week—rest days are important for avoiding injury—but I strongly suggest on your day off that you move your body with a walk and some simple stretching.

If you're thinking, "But working out just isn't my thing," experience tells me you haven't found the type of exercise that is right *for you*. When people ask me for the best kind of exercise for various results—whether it's to get stronger, lose weight, or get healthier overall—my answer is always the same: "The best exercise is the kind of exercise you will actually do."

Sure, I can tell you that HIIT (high intensity interval training) is the most effective to burn fat and build lean muscle in the least amount of time, but if you hate doing it, guess what? You won't do it. If you despise doing something, what are the chances you will stick to it? About zero. The solution is to find what works for you, not your skinny friend, your triathlete brother, or a celebrity on TikTok. And don't limit your notions of exercise to running or Pilates. Ballroom dancing (or any kind of dancing, including hip-hop dancing in your living room), walking your dog for longer distances, pickleball, riding your bike or walking instead of driving, ice skating, horseback riding, gardening, hiking—just get out there. Here are some tips to make it happen:

- **Find what moves you—literally—and make it a habit.** The more habitual the exercise is, the less brain power you will need to consistently do it, because there will be less friction between making excuses not to work out and putting on your gear and getting started. It will become a natural thing you do on a regular basis. To figure out what types of exercise you like the most (or hate the least), I suggest trying a bunch of different things. As the old saying goes, "You need to kiss a lot of frogs to find that prince," and the same is true for exercise. I really like weight training and running. Even though I do other things, I always gravitate back to those two forms of exercise.

- **Keep it simple.** One good thing that came out of the pandemic is how many people working from home found they had more time to work out from home too. Some began to exercise regularly for the first time. Did you hop on this trend? Can you work out from home instead of driving to a gym? It's so easy now to order up equipment and have it delivered to your door, and to find low-cost online classes or apps to help you get started and keep going. If having to drive somewhere to work out is what stops you from working out, remove that barrier with a simple solution: exercise at home.

- **Sweat with a friend.** A great way to get started with an exercise routine and keep going is to recruit an accountability buddy to keep you on course. Make a date with a pal for a regularly scheduled morning, afternoon, or evening walk or bike ride, or make it a family affair. Sign yourself up for a 5K run that you'll want to train for and then check out running or walking clubs offered at your local YMCA or community center, or even at retail outlets like running-gear stores. I've railed against how much time we can waste scrolling through social media, but there are some good apps like MapMyWalk where you can connect with other "friends" who have exercise goals.

- **Focus on consistency over intensity.** That's what I tell clients all the time when we're training. Yes, you should push yourself to the next level—and a harder workout will help you get there. But don't make this mistake: You are doing an intense workout and giving it your all, but you only are doing it twice a week. If you destroy yourself every time you work out, you won't want to do it regularly. Your brain and your body are much better off if you substitute sporadic intensity with everyday consistency. Sure, you should aim for bigger, better, and bolder when it comes to exercise—but build up to it. Give it your all—but do it gradually so you don't just give up. And here's a pro tip: Listen to your body to avoid pushing yourself into an injury. If it hurts, stop. Personally, as long as I sweat every day and get my heart rate up for a good thirty minutes, I'm thrilled. That's enough for me to get the physical and cognitive benefits I crave.

Bold Spirit Rituals

Call the Spin Doctor

We all have about 6,200 thoughts a day, 80 percent of which are negative thoughts! That's a lot of negative thinking, the type of thinking that can hold us back from positive pursuits. For those with a tendency toward anxiety or depression, 95 percent of those negative thoughts are on "repeat play," something cognitive behavioral psychologists refer to as "automatic negative thinking."

Negative thoughts can take on many forms, but we can practice new habits for positive, productive thoughts. Here are a few ideas for flipping the script on negative thinking, followed by my tips for looking at things a different way, with a positive spin.

If you tend to overgeneralize and take things personally . . .

Negative Thinking: *I matched with the one and only guy on the dating app I thought was cute and he ghosted me. That's it. There's no one out there for me.*

Positive Spin: Look out for the "absolutes" in your statements. Instead of deciding there is "no one" out there, try: *This guy wasn't "the one" but I can swipe again tomorrow.*

If you tell yourself off for making a bad choice . . .

Negative Thinking: *Why did I binge the entire new season of that show and go to bed at 3:30 a.m. when I have to get to work early today? I'm such a moron!*

Positive Spin: Be kind to yourself and put things into perspective. Try: *It's not the end of the world. Who hasn't binge-watched something? Besides, I liked it! But I'll show myself some love by getting the sleep I deserve tonight and being more on point at work tomorrow.*

If you feel guilty for losing control . . .

Negative Thinking: *I can't believe I ate all those donuts for breakfast and then gave into my craving for chips. I even blew off my workout! Why can't I clean up my act?*

Positive Spin: Forgive yourself and move on. Try: *Tomorrow is another chance to get this right. I will remind myself that I always feel so much better when I exercise and eat well. My health is important. One "bad" day doesn't mean I won't reach my goals.*

If you focus on the negative even when good things happen . . .

Negative Thinking: *I got the last seat on the red-eye so I could surprise my girlfriend on her birthday, but they gave me the damn middle seat, in the last row near the stinky bathroom. This flight sucks.*

Positive Spin: Lean into the happy part of the situation. Try: *Clearly, there's nothing that will stop me from seeing my girlfriend on her birthday. I can't wait to hold her in my arms.*

If you are often critical of other people . . .

Negative Thinking: *My coworker is always brownnosing our boss and getting her to agree to everything she asks for. She got to leave early again for her kid's soccer game, and now she's going on the New York trip to give the big presentation. She asks, she gets. She's a shark and my boss is a doormat.*

Positive Spin: Look for positive attributes in others. Try: *My coworker is pretty bold. She asks for what she wants and, lo and behold, she gets it. Seems like my boss is trying to create a healthy work environment. Maybe I should ask for a few things too. Can't hurt to try. What's the worst that can happen?*

We can't get rid of all our negative thoughts, but we can practice trying to be more positive, especially in the areas where we find ourselves being most negative. Positivity attracts positive things.

THE POSITIVE POWER OF NEGATIVE VISUALIZATION

You read that right—negative thinking has an upside, but this technique depends on your perspective.

Catastrophizing is when you imagine the worst, even when there is no evidence of the worst becoming reality. People catastrophize when their spouse isn't answering their texts while on a business trip, when they are waiting for routine medical test results, or when the company they are trying to do a deal with postpones their meeting. But there's a difference between a "what can go wrong, will go wrong" mentality and the practice of negative visualization, where we proactively imagine worst-case scenarios as if they are happening right then and there. It's a coping habit that dates back to the Stoics.

I learned about negative visualization when I had Amanda Knox as a guest on my *Habits & Hustle* podcast. As you may recall, Knox was a twenty-year-old exchange student in Italy when her roommate, Meredith Kercher, was found brutally murdered in their apartment. Knox spent four years in an Italian prison, convicted for a crime she didn't commit. (She was officially acquitted in 2015.)

Knox shared how she was able to get through each day by using negative visualization to imagine the worst-case scenario. By thinking of all the ways things could go wrong for her, whether in legal proceedings or her daily life behind bars, Knox was able to make it through to the other side with a sense of relief instead of dread, even when the worst case became reality.

Negative visualization psychologically prepares even the boldest among us for potential bad outcomes and whatever life throws our way. We are primed and ready to accept and deal with our new reality. The practice helps us overcome our greatest fears, or at least lessen their impact. And when the worst-case scenario does not transpire, we are even more grateful for it.

Try Meditation

I find meditation challenging. I have tried a few methods and it's quite difficult for me to quiet my mind that way, but I've read enough about the practice and have heard from so many meditators that I believe its benefits are real. Have you tried it? Meditation, according to many studies, can slow your heart rate, lower your blood pressure, reduce stress, and even enhance your immune function, among other things. The "relaxation response" associated with meditation is well-documented.

Those who adopt a meditation practice say that the mental clarity they get from it frees them from extraneous thoughts, worries, and concerns that distract them from focusing on the task at hand. A work-from-home friend, which is almost everyone I know these days, told me that when she is having a hectic morning with her young kids and feeling totally frazzled before going to her computer for yet another conference call, she closes her door, and then her eyes, and practices a few minutes of mindful meditation before she logs on. She swears she can better concentrate on the call—and whatever comes up next when she opens the door again and faces her kids.

You can practice meditation on your own time, without any special equipment. You can do it at home, at your desk at work, or even on the train on the way to the office. There are many wonderful books, apps, and online classes on meditation, or you might live in a city where drop-in meditation centers proliferate. Community centers, the local Y, libraries, and hospitals often offer free or low-cost classes if you're looking for instruction beyond what you can access on your own.

Meditation can help you become more mindful of what's transpiring inside you and around you. Instead of thinking about how to respond to a social media post or something a coworker did that irked you, a daily meditation practice will train your brain to let those thoughts pass you by instead of wasting your precious brain power thinking about how to react. Some studies have shown that mindfulness can weaken negative thoughts, while others have found that meditation can help attenuate self-defeating and self-deprecating thoughts. Meditation can help us become not only less judgmental of ourselves, but also less judgmental of others. And when we're not allocating time to second-guessing our abilities—or criticizing others' abilities—we can focus on moving forward.

Given all the benefits of meditation, I am still trying to find ways to make it a part of my daily life. And who knows? Maybe by the time you read this, it will be.

DIY: Self-Hypnosis

As humans, we have a superpower. We can change the way we think. Our unconscious mind has a stronger effect over our behavior than we realize. Hypnotherapy taps into brain networks to enable us to change the way we think and experience the world around us.

Four decades of research and clinical experience by psychiatrist Dr. David Spiegel—the foremost expert on self-hypnosis and director of the Stanford Center on Stress and Health—have shown that self-hypnosis can help focus our current state of mind. It helps us "decrease distracting thoughts and sensations" while opening us to new ideas and perspectives. Self-hypnosis has also been shown to help improve the way we manage stress, pain, insomnia, and even tough addictions like smoking.

If you think self-hypnosis may be right for you, there are several popular digital hypnosis apps available to try, such as HypnoBox, as well as many books and online resources. Some apps and online programs are specifically designed to help users with specific goals, such as quitting smoking or weight loss, so look for something more general to start.

Sleep Better, Dream Bolder

Getting a good night's sleep is vital for focus, learning new things, mood regulation, and productivity, which are all important factors for taking a big, bold leap and for being resilient enough to get back up again when we fail.

A bad night's sleep makes it really tough to be as sharp and focused the next day as we need to be. And when we are sleep-deprived, it's very difficult to focus on tasks and learn a new skill.

It's important to keep your circadian rhythm on track by going to bed and waking up at the same time every day, even on weekends. When our circadian rhythm is out of whack, we tend to feel exhausted and lethargic—jet lag, minus the jet. We get less done on our to-do lists. We lean toward grabbing quick-and-easy comfort foods that aren't healthy, leading to more lethargy and weight gain. If our circadian rhythm is constantly off cycle, we are more susceptible to mental disorders and physical illness.

To maintain your circadian rhythm, sleep experts recommend getting natural light exposure first thing in the morning and dimming the lights at night as bedtime approaches. Other common-sense tips: cut out your afternoon caffeine, refrain from staring into the phone and laptop screens a couple of hours before bed, and sleep in a cool, dark room.

But we're not all wired the same way, and you may actually have more energy later in the day, or perhaps you have a job where you work a night shift. If you're a health-care worker or in the restaurant industry, or if your business requires you to work in more than one time zone, you rarely work nine to five.

Understanding your natural circadian rhythm for more focus during the day (whatever hours you keep) will depend on your "chronotype," which is an individual's propensity to sleep at certain times. Dr. Michael Breus, PhD, aka "the Sleep Doctor" and author of *The Power of When: Discover Your Chronotype—and the Best Time to Eat Lunch, Ask for a Raise, Have Sex, Write a Novel, Take Your Meds, and More,* was a guest on *Habits & Hustle* and introduced me to his four chronotypes—dolphin, lion, bear, and wolf—each with their own sleep schedule and habits.

Depending on your chronotype, he says, you tend to sleep between certain hours of the twenty-four-hour cycle. When awake, you also tend to have more focus in certain windows of the day. For some, morning hours are their most productive. For others, nighttime is when focus is heightened. Identifying your sleep chronotype can set you up for a more productive day. To discover your chronotype, I recommend taking this quiz: https://thepowerofwhen quiz.com/.

Good sleep hygiene also heightens our ability to learn new things. Sleep plays a role in what's called the "consolidation of memory," which enables us to learn something, practice it over a period of time, and lock it into our memory to retrieve it when we need it, even years later. The better we sleep, the better we're able to retain new information, and the longer we're able to retrieve it.

Finally, a good night's sleep can elevate your mood. While you sleep, your brain is processing your emotions. If a night's sleep is cut short, so is the brain's ability to sort through your emotions fully, and you'll likely feel a little cranky and impatient the next day.

It's nearly impossible to feel bold when you're not well rested. Add a regular sleep regimen to your practice and wake up on the bold side of the bed each day.

Test the Personal Energy Allocation Theory

It's 4:30 p.m. on a Tuesday and you have to make a vital decision on a work project by 5:00 p.m. You've been making decisions all day long, from what to wear to work, to which new ad copy works best, to what to get for lunch in the cafeteria, to which new vendor to contract. And by the time the most important decision of the day is on your desk, your energy is drained and you can't think straight.

You have "decision fatigue," a term coined by social psychologist Roy Baumeister. Studies show that Americans make a whopping thirty-five thousand decisions a day. Some of these decisions are so small or routine that we don't think of them as decisions, like choosing your shoes for work or what toppings you want on your pizza. When we've made thousands of decisions earlier in the day, by the time 4:30 rolls around and we are asked to make a big decision, it can feel like our brain has already packed up and gone home. We've run out of energy.

Each of us has only so much energy in a given day and, while we know that big tasks can sap our energy, even little decisions require some of our daily energy expenditure. We can use our energy on making big, bold moves, or we can waste it on a million tiny things that add up to very little in the end. I realized that I could avoid decision fatigue by properly allocating the energy I spent on decision-making from the moment I wake up in the morning to the minute I go to sleep at night. I call it the Personal Energy Allocation.

I think of the brain like a drawer. We can either overstuff it by spending time on insignificant things like what to wear or what to eat for breakfast, or we can follow a daily pattern and process that works on autopilot, leaving the drawer neat and organized. I've automated and simplified my routines wherever possible.

My work life keeps me on my toes. It can be hectic, and the things I'm focused on can change day-to-day. One minute I'm working with clients on their brand strategy, the next I'm preparing for a podcast by doing some research and reading up on my guest, and the next I'm following up with a potential sponsor for a client of mine. Throughout, my kids are always my top two priorities. Balancing where I put my focus means allocating my energy only on what's important.

Here's how I put my daily Personal Energy Allocation to work for me: Before I go to bed, I make sure the heat or A/C in my room is set to the temperature best for a great night's sleep (cool but not cold). I put a glass of water on my nightstand that I'll drink before I get out of bed in the morning. When I wake up, I get into my workout clothes and running shoes. I make myself the same breakfast each morning and then I spend about ten minutes checking my email to make sure there's nothing urgent I need to respond to, skipping emails that don't need immediate attention. I get my kids their breakfast and take them to school. Once I'm back home, I do my daily workout, shower, dress in my usual jeans, and start my workday.

While nothing about my personal routine is earth-shattering, the point is this: I make very few decisions before my workday begins, conserving as much energy as I can for the more complex decisions I have to make while I work. If there's an important decision to make by 5:00 p.m., I am as sharp as I can be.

Big, bold decision-making requires your full attention. Dump the distractions and up your brain power by designing your own Personal Energy Allocation. Here are some energy-saving tips based on my own routine.

Choose Your Uniform

Unless it's a special occasion, I keep my wardrobe choices super simple so that I don't spend energy digging in my closet or staring in the mirror. I wear a variation of the same outfit every day. I have a few pairs of jeans and lots of leggings that I mix and match with various shirts depending on the weather. If you work from home, streamlining your choices should be a quick fix. If you work in a less casual environment, gather some basics that suit you and put them to work, at work.

Plan Your Meals

When you meal plan and do a little prep, you eat better and save time. You're not tempted to get takeout on the way home from work or eat a box of sugary cereal for dinner. I create a specific menu for each meal—breakfast, lunch, and even dinner with my family. If this sounds overwhelming (especially if you have kids), start with the one meal of the day that is easiest for you to control. Maybe that's breakfast, where less cooking is generally involved. I eat mine solo while my kids are getting ready for school. If breakfast is always rushed and lunch is at your desk, then focus on planning dinner.

Stick to a Sleep Routine

I go to bed and wake up at the same time every day. I'm in bed by around 10:30 p.m. and wake up at 6:30 a.m., even on the weekends. (OK, not all weekends, but most weekends!) Figure out your own sleep schedule—which we've just discussed—stick to it, and recoup some personal energy.

Get Up and Move

I rarely sit still. Sitting in front of a computer for a Zoom meeting is a total energy suck, and I avoid it as often as I can, especially when it's an hour-long meeting with ten minutes of value. Can you swap out a meeting with a productive phone call or an email exchange? We are spending way too much time on video conferencing, and chances are your colleagues and boss would agree.

Get off Zoom and get outside, if at all possible. I make all my calls while walking outside or on the treadmill. I've often invited my guests to walk on the treadmill next to mine while recording my podcast. Research shows that physical movement fuels our creativity and problem-solving capabilities by 80 to 100 percent, boosts our productivity at work, reduces mental fatigue, and helps us focus our attention and stay on task.

If you can't walk while you work—and that may be impossible in your job—I understand. Not everyone lives in sunny California or has a boss who'd be OK with a walk-and-talk approach. But get up and move during the workday. Sitting in front of your computer for hours on end is a bold killer. Try a standing desk or even a treadmill desk. Set a timer or use an app so that you get up and move every forty-five minutes. You're expending energy to increase your energy!

And if you can get outdoors and into the fresh air during the workday, do it. Even a ten-minute walk outside can add the energy you need to power you through your next task. Many corporations and even smaller companies have gotten more progressive in creating work environments that are wellness friendly. They are seeing the value in having a less sedentary workforce, and programs like running or walking clubs (or even on-site classes and workout spaces, if you're lucky) build camaraderie as they increase wellness. Take advantage of these perks, or if there is nothing like this in your workplace, consider suggesting that your company explore these options—a bold and beneficial move.

Do the Hard Stuff First

When you begin the day with dread in your head—with tasks that you just don't want to do because they are difficult, uncomfortable, or even boring—it can weigh you down all day long. Whether it's putting together a proposal, making a difficult phone call, or finalizing that spreadsheet report, I recommend doing whatever you're avoiding first. Get it off your plate and out of your consciousness so that you can free up your bold brain energy.

The hard stuff is often what keeps us up at night because we know it's important to get it done and out of the way to reach our goals. The hard stuff is the stuff that we make worse by putting it off for days, maybe weeks. It's the stuff we *know* needs to be tackled first, and too often it's the job that gets moved down the list, day after day.

If you're struggling with this, try to pinpoint what's stopping you. If you need help, ask for it. Asking for what you want is the ultimate bold move, as is asking for what you *need*. Are you hesitating because it will cost you time and money? Are you waiting on someone else to do something before you can tackle the task? Are you just procrastinating because it's boring (but essential)? Depending on the task, you might be able to knock it off your list with my 3Fs Method (Principle #12). Take a peek ahead, if you want, but the 3Fs aren't an excuse or an exemption—they're just a tool for dealing with the hard stuff.

I think of it this way: The time we spend making excuses is time we're wasting on not getting shit done! And the crazy thing is that getting the hard stuff done means we can get *more important* shit done! I learned this the hard way, as my family and my business grew simultaneously. But knocking the hard stuff off my list first thing improved my overall decision-making and my determination.

I am a creature of habit, a stickler for routine, and a believer in daily rituals. I also know that life is unpredictable and sometimes we have to be a little flexible. The alarm doesn't go off, your company is sold, a tree falls on your roof, your mom gets sick, the kids are sick, or you wake up with a sore throat. Life happens. But in general, having a daily go-to routine will energize your body and fuel your brain, and when life does throw you a curveball, a routine will help you get back on track. Bold habits keep your bold muscles warmed up and ready to go when you need them!

Principle #6

Don't Stop Before You Start

TO FORM ANY NEW HABIT, we must first overcome any resistance to getting started. Whether it's a general lack of motivation, fatigue, anxiety, fear, or any other negative mindset, or just a practical roadblock like your hectic schedule, the more energy we need to clear those hurdles and take action, the harder it is to get going on your bold journey.

That's why I've just given you the tools to make habit building a little easier. Going from good (or even not so good) to better to bigger to bold and living that richer life starts with self-efficacy—the belief that *you can do this*. Hit the reset button on your mindset with the Principles you've learned so far, and then reinforce that mental shift with bold habits that you'll practice every day—whether it's sticking to that daily walk or knocking the hardest thing off your to-do list first thing. I can tell you to do all this, but now it's in your hands to train your brain to be bold.

I can't make you do it. I can only point you in the right direction and give you a road map. You're on the precipice now and it's time to jump. If you're ready to go for it, skip to the next Principle. But if you need one more push, here's a little story that I hope might inspire you.

Habit and Hustle: My Own Journey

Maybe you can relate to how I felt as a kid, especially during those adolescent years. Not smart enough. Not attractive enough. Not cool enough. A walking, talking bundle of self-doubt. I was also shy. Except . . . for some reason I leaned into scrappy and relentless.

Maybe it was that Gen X "figure it out for yourself" thing, or maybe it was being raised for a while by a single mom, recalling her financial struggles and vowing I wouldn't go through that myself. Maybe I never got over being told I was "average, at best," or I just wanted spending money for the mall. (At one point I worked three part-time jobs—not because I needed the money to feed myself, but because I wanted the freedom that came with having my own money, which symbolized independence.) Whatever did it, something sparked inside of me and pushed me off the starting block, and I was motivated to be bold, to ask for what I wanted.

But I stalled out and hesitated, many times. (And I admit, sometimes I still feel that way.) I nearly stopped before I got started, because I couldn't silence that little voice: *You can't do it.*

In the end, it always came back to one thing: sticking to my bold mindset and the daily habits that reinforce it. As I got older, those habits grew up with me. Here's how one of those practices—a simple daily workout—developed over the years, from a habit to a part of my identity.

It was a rite of passage in my town for Jewish high school girls to join the Chai Folk Ensemble, the prestigious Israeli dance troupe that remains internationally recognized today. Among my crowd, if you were not part of Chai, as we called it, you weren't part of life. You missed out on all the fun, all the gossip, all the post-rehearsal get-togethers, all the after-parties, all of it. I imagine it's what teenagers would be going through today if they didn't have phones and all their friends did, or if they didn't have access to their friends' Instagram or TikTok accounts or whatever the next big social media thing is by the time you read this. Well, that was me. I flunked the audition and didn't make the troupe. I was out.

To be honest, I've always been terrible at dancing, and I remember feeling particularly insecure and out of my league the day I tried out for Chai. I was missing steps, I wasn't keeping the beat, I moved left when others moved right . . . I was awful, and I left the audition feeling embarrassed for even considering trying out. Though it shouldn't have come as a shock when I heard I hadn't made it, I was devastated. Not only would I be missing out on what all my friends were doing after school together, but I'd have to find something to keep myself busy and distracted while they were learning some supercool (I was sure) Israeli hora dance moves.

When that door slammed shut, I decided then and there that I'd go jiggle the knob on another one, or find an open window. As it turns out, an all-women's gym called Shapes had opened just down the street from our house. When I didn't get into Chai, I joined Shapes, and it became my place to go when everyone was at rehearsal, between school and dinnertime. This was the heyday of Jane Fonda, Denise Austin, and Richard Simmons, and the aerobics classes I took proved to be a different kind of dancing—one that I could do quite well. I fell in love with the feeling I got after I went to Shapes.

Sometimes, when I got home from school, I didn't feel like going. *I'm too tired to work out. Everyone else is at rehearsal having fun. I don't want to go. It's too much trouble.* I wanted to sink into my couch with a snack and watch TV. But I pushed through it. I had to remind myself that I *always* felt better when I went to class, no matter how unmotivated and crappy I felt when I got home from school. So, I kept at it, lacing up my Reebok high-tops and running over to Shapes. And week by week, step-by-step, I noticed incremental improvements in my body and in my brain.

While I was never overweight, I was, as my grandmother would say, zaftig (Yiddish for having a round figure). Once I went all-in at the gym, my body changed. I became strong and muscular, and I liked it. But more importantly, I was feeling stronger mentally. Fitness built my confidence and self-esteem. It made me more disciplined. I became more open to challenging myself and trying new things. Whatever insecurities I had, whatever I didn't like about myself or wanted to improve, physically or mentally, fitness was proving to be the answer.

Twenty-five years later, I had my own fitness DVD series, Jane Fonda hired *me* for a project, and I became friends with Denise Austin. I also became a trainer on a hit reality show, as well as a trainer to pop stars and world-class athletes, wrote two books on fitness, and launched a fitness-inspired shoe company. I failed that Chai audition, but I got something better.

Your Habits Fuel Your Hustle

Fitness was not just a habit; it became a part of my identity. The more I practiced the habit of fitness, the more I identified as a fitness person. The same transformation can occur for you, when you practice so-called identity-based habits. In other words, if you practice bold habits, you will become a bold person.

If you are struggling with adopting your new bold habits, it could be that "limbic friction" in your brain is throwing up a roadblock for your body. Limbic friction is how neuroscientists describe the gap between *wanting* to do a thing and actually *doing* that thing. But you can kick it to the curb with a few simple fixes.

Let's say you want to set a new habit of getting up an hour earlier each day to go to the gym, meditate, or write a few pages of your first novel before heading to work. But when the alarm goes off at 5:30 a.m., it's painful. It takes everything you've got not to keep pressing the snooze button or turn off the alarm and go back to sleep. That strain of getting up earlier than usual is limbic friction—it's like a war between your intellectual self and your physical self. And limbic friction is generally what keeps us from pursuing our goals. The best way to overcome limbic friction is to set linchpin habits in place that help override it. In the example of getting up an hour earlier, a linchpin habit would be to start going to bed an hour earlier to offset the earlier wake time. Curbing caffeine intake is a linchpin habit for going to bed earlier and being able to fall asleep and remain asleep. Setting up your workout gear, your meditation space, or your writing nook before you go to bed are examples of linchpin habits that can help you get straight to your morning tasks. It's really that simple. What linchpin habit could help you reach your goal?

Once we can overcome resistance to building a new habit, the goal is to practice that habit consistently and repeatedly over time until it feels like a completely natural part of our lives, just like brushing our teeth. This is neuroplasticity in action: the process of hardwiring a habit into our brain so that it becomes reflexive.

Experiences change the brain. If you want that bigger, better life, push yourself off that wall you've been sitting on for far too long and practice habits that will lead you to a bold identity. What are you waiting for?

PART 3

BOLDNESS IS A SKILL

Choose a Direction, Not a Destination

THE BOLD LIFE IS A journey. It's not just about a goal.

When we are set on reaching a specific destination—like a promotion, a magic number of dollars in a retirement account, or a milestone in our personal lives such as finally starting a family or moving to a new city—we inevitably encounter challenges along the way. Sometimes the challenges alert us to whether our direction is serving us well. Sometimes we discover a new idea or opportunity we never expected and change directions. And sometimes, circumstances beyond our control make a destination unattainable. We need to pivot.

My life and career have taken me places I never expected to be, introduced me to people I never expected to meet, and led me on adventures I never expected to take. And yet, my life and career have always been moving forward, even when—especially when—I pivoted in a new direction. I've pivoted again and again, sometimes by choice, sometimes propelled by circumstances beyond my control. The one constant is my self-efficacy—my belief in my capabilities—no matter the direction I take, or where my life takes me. It's more important to have confidence in yourself than assurance of reaching a specific destination.

Jennifer Hudson's story is a great illustration of self-efficacy, and of trusting that you're moving in the right direction. The singer and actress first became well-known in 2004, when she was a contestant on the third season of Fox's *American Idol* and her voice stunned the judges. It was a shock to all, including Hudson, when she was eliminated early, placing seventh. That was hardly the end of the road for her. Straight off her *American Idol* elimination, Hudson landed the role of Effie White in *Dreamgirls*, winning an Academy Award for her performance. Around that time, she was signed by Arista Records and released her self-titled first album, which went gold. In the years since, her success as both a musical artist and film actress has been stupendous.

But what would have happened to Hudson's career had she won *American Idol*? She would have been contractually obligated to record an album, tour, and whatever else American Idols do. She may not have been able to audition for *Dreamgirls*. She would likely have had to release an album dictated by her *Idol* contract, and which she may not have wanted to put her name on.

Jennifer Hudson's early elimination could have derailed her career had she believed that winning *American Idol* was her best hope for success. But thankfully, she didn't and it wasn't. She accepted that her destination was still undetermined. And it turned out that her failure provided her with a winning direction. Even though she lost, the casting team for *Dreamgirls* had noticed her, which led to an audition. Without being eliminated from *American Idol*, she likely would never have gotten the opportunities she did. Hudson never regretted her shot at *American Idol*, though she didn't win.

Direction is much more consequential to a rich life than the goals and destinations we choose. Here are some tips for navigating your bold path, even when you think you're lost.

Connect the Dots Life Hands You— but First Collect Them

Think of all the times things didn't work out the way you planned, for better or for worse. Now, perhaps, you can appreciate how you were always moving in the right direction. As the late Apple founder and CEO Steve Jobs said in his commencement speech to Stanford University's class of 2005, we may not be able to see it at the time, but when we look back, it's all very clear how the "dots"—those experiences in our lives, great and small—connect.

In his speech, Jobs, who famously did not graduate from college, talks about how his status as a dropout led to something he never expected. Reed College, he explains, was famous for its calligraphy instruction. "Throughout the campus, every poster, every label on every drawer, was beautifully hand calligraphed. Because I had dropped out and didn't have to take the normal classes, I decided to take a calligraphy class to learn how to do this. I learned about serif and sans serif typefaces, about varying the amount of space between different letter combinations, about what makes great typography great. It was beautiful, historical, artistically subtle in a way that science can't capture, and I found it fascinating," he said.

He never dreamed his brief foray into calligraphy would figure into his future plans, but ten years later, when Jobs was designing the first Macintosh computer, his experience came back to influence him in a big way. "It was the first computer with beautiful typography. If I had never dropped in on that single course in college, the Mac would have never had multiple typefaces or proportionally spaced fonts. And since Windows just copied the Mac, it's likely that no personal computer would have them."

If Steve Jobs hadn't dropped out, he wouldn't have been able to take that calligraphy class that inspired the iconic designs of all Apple products, as well as virtually every personal computer in use today. "Of course it was impossible to connect the dots looking forward when I was in college. But it was very, very clear looking backward ten years later," he told the graduates.

When you trust that the "dots"—a job you didn't get, a detour you took to a different city, a flat tire, whatever it may be—will somehow connect in your future, your direction will emerge. If you let go of focusing on a single destination, your journey becomes bigger, better, and bolder.

To be bold means to collect all the life experiences—the dots—that fuel your personal growth, and those include failures as well as successes. Even when you're handed a disappointing outcome, collect that dot, because it will have value later on. As long as you're still in motion, taking action, you're moving forward. The alternative is not trying at all, and that won't get you anywhere. So even if you fail, even if you think things are moving in the opposite direction because you don't get what you want, even if failure causes you to detour or even derail, just press on. It may take months, years, even a decade or more, but at some point you'll be able to look back, like Jennifer Hudson or Steve Jobs, and see how all the dots you *collected* ultimately *connected*.

Don't Be Afraid to Go Off-Road

A few years ago, I had a production deal for a television show I'd sold called *Game Changers*, where we'd peek into the lives of highly successful people who were the best in their fields— the thought leaders, major disruptors, and individuals who were just overall extraordinary. I wanted it to be a "day in the life"—what time they woke up, what they ate, all their daily rituals, habits, and routines. The objective was for viewers to get practical takeaways they could integrate into their lives.

The development deal was in place, we had a green light for the pilot, and we were on the brink of getting everything signed, sealed, and delivered and rolling those cameras, but . . . but . . . but . . . we absolutely couldn't work out the details. Let's just say the production company had very different ideas on who I should interview. I wanted the greatest minds of today and they—well, they wanted something else more celebrity oriented. One month of negotiations turned into two months, then three, then six, then more than a year. And finally, after being stuck at a crossroads for more than a year, I decided to walk away. But as I collected this big fat dot, I saw a major opportunity. I believed in my idea and wanted to bring it to life somehow, but I realized my concept didn't need to be turned into a TV show; it could easily be tweaked into a podcast format. Soon after that, I launched a weekly podcast called *Habits & Hustle*, which gets millions of downloads, and eventually partnered with Entrepreneur Media. I am doing exactly what I wanted to do with the TV show—and actually it's better than TV because I have so much more freedom. I spend hours interviewing fascinating people and thought leaders: major figures across a broad spectrum of fields like self-help guru Tony Robbins, actor and producer Matthew McConaughey, makeup maven

Bobbi Brown, and so many others who candidly share lessons on success with my ever-growing audience.

I thought my destination was to have a TV show. But that failure caused me to change course—and that new direction led me to the real prize.

Do Bring a Map

I've been telling you that you should be open to taking a detour or going off your path altogether, that your direction is more important than your destination. But that's not to say that you shouldn't set out on your bold journey knowing where you'd like to wind up. I want you to be flexible, resilient, comfortable with failure, and ready to pivot if you need to, but having a general direction is important, even if it's just "up" or "straight ahead"! On the other side of that "up" or "straight ahead," you should have a goal in mind, and a plan for achieving it.

A general direction is good, but a destination too broadly defined (as in, *I just want to be happy . . . I just want to be successful . . . I just want love . . .*) can trip you up. You may not achieve your goals if they're too vague, and you could even be back to square one—settling for what you get, rather than chasing what you really want. Rather than chase lots of wants, zero in on one thing for now. And then you can design your own road map—with the understanding that you may need to pivot and switch direction along the way.

If you're still in need of some clarity about what you want (and how you can get it), try asking yourself these questions and use the answers to draw your map.

- Why do you want this?

- How will it improve your life?

- When do you want it, or is that not a consideration?

- How will you get it?

- Who (or what) can help you?

My hope is that you have already started to answer some of these questions, and that you've been practicing the skills we discussed earlier—like asking for something small, just to get your feet wet—to build up your bold muscles.

Sara Blakely, the billionaire founder of Spanx, had a plan to get what she wanted and, most importantly, she executed every move with boldness. But she didn't necessarily have those specific steps in mind when she came up with her road map. She had to think fast many times and pivot as needed, but her flexibility and resilience paid off.

Blakely was selling fax machines in the late 1990s when she had the idea for her footless, body-shaping pantyhose, but she had no expertise in that industry and little funding for a start-up. Still, Blakely believed in herself and in her idea (self-efficacy in action!), and she took her concept from mill to mill until she found a hosiery manufacturer willing to produce the product—because his daughters said that it was a great idea.

When her first samples were ready, she cold-called Neiman Marcus to pitch Spanx, offering to fly to their Dallas headquarters. After persisting with many calls, she scored a ten-minute meeting. Selling fax machines—and getting rejected in the process—was a dot that Blakely had collected early in her career, and she connected it to other dots as she was building her company. Pitching a piece of office equipment was different than selling body-shaping apparel, but it was still sales. "I knew from selling fax machines that you don't leave a message," she said in 2018 at the Goldman Sachs 10,000 Small Businesses Summit.

When the female buyer's interest seemed to wane five minutes into the pitch, Blakely knew she had to change her tactics and pivot, fast. She asked the buyer to come with her into the women's bathroom. And yes, this buyer's eyebrows rose and she said, "Excuse me?" But she agreed, and Blakely slipped into a stall where she did a quick-change before-and-after demo of the transformative power of her product, modeling how her white pants looked without the Spanx, and then with them. If you're a woman who's ever attempted to wear light-colored pants with confidence, then you'll understand why the buyer was immediately impressed! She ordered Spanx for seven Neiman's stores on the spot, and Blakely's invention took off—so fast and so far that in

2012 *Forbes* declared her the world's youngest self-made female billionaire.

Sara Blakely's plan likely did not include conducting the most important part of her presentation in the women's bathroom. But she knew she needed to switch gears to save her pitch, and it worked. In her 2019 MasterClass, Blakely says that a common misconception about successful people who get what they go after is "that we had it all figured out before we even took the leap. That is not the case at all. . . . The main thing I've learned from being an entrepreneur is you just learn as you go."

Your destination may not be entrepreneurial in nature, but, as Blakely says, "If you're waiting until you've got it all figured out, you're going to be waiting forever."

Don't wait.

Know the Difference
Between a Big Risk and a Bold Move

Bold people start, ready or not. Here's the truth: we're rarely 100 percent ready for anything new in life. You can be physically prepared with all the right gear to climb a mountain, but are you mentally ready for every aspect of the adventure, from the fear of sustaining injury (or worse) to the thrill of reaching the top? Maybe not, but it's your dream and you go anyway! You can be physically ready to start a family, but once that newborn baby arrives there will be plenty of moments (24-7) that take you by surprise. Do you balk when you stop and think about what could go wrong? Nope, you have always wanted to be a parent, and besides, you're in the delivery room!

Now, you may be ready (mentally and physically) to start that small business you've been thinking about, until someone asks you this: *Are you ready to take a risk?* They will ask you to stop and consider all the things you can lose: Money! Time! Reputation!

Here is something very important to keep in mind when you share your bold idea in search of constructive feedback: know your audience, and consider the source. For example, let's say you're trying to launch that little company that's been your dream for years. So, don't spill your guts to someone who thinks starting a small business is a horrible idea and that you should stick with working for a big corporation complete with benefits and a 401(k) plan, and don't share your big dream with a small-minded person. Share your wish with a non-skeptic who will appreciate your vision—even better, with someone who has done something similar. Don't ask someone for advice on something they've never done before and expect to get total buy-in plus no-fail tips. That seems like an obvious thing to avoid, but many of us make this mistake all the time.

People have all sorts of reasons and motives for telling you why you should or shouldn't do something. Many of those closest to you don't want to see you get hurt. Perhaps your parents, for instance, don't want to see their child fail, even (sometimes especially) if you are an adult. They care about what happens to you, and their reservations are completely unselfish. But the naysayers may have other motives. An older sibling (the "responsible" one) who tries to stop you may be inwardly groaning that she'll have to be the one to clean up your emotional and financial mess if your venture doesn't pan out. A former colleague may tell you your business is a terrible idea because he's jealous that you thought of it first.

Even a good friend may not want to see you succeed. If they don't have the guts to make a bold move, you doing so (and being successful at it!) will make them regret not taking the leap as well. They may feel like they're failing, so they'd rather you stick to the status quo, whether they are aware that this is their intention or not. So, friends and family may warn you that your idea is too scary: "It's not worth it." "Are you sure you want to take that risk?" "Seems like a big gamble to me. I wouldn't do it if I were you . . . "

To be honest, I don't want you to take a risk either. Nope, not even me. But I do want you to be *bold*. There's a difference between taking a risk and making a big, bold move. Understanding the difference before you get started is key.

Risk is a win-lose equation, a zero-sum, either-or kind of game. Either you'll win at everything or lose everything. Let's use the example of opening a restaurant, which is one of the hardest things to do in any economy. But this is it. This is the one thing you want.

Taking a risk means that if the restaurant fails, you'll wind up worse off. You may be in debt. You may become depressed. You may have to live with your parents. Your partner may leave you. Risk leaves you with little reward.

On the other hand, being bold is a win-win equation. Being bold is understanding that even though there is a risk that the restaurant will fail, you've done everything you can to safeguard yourself:

- You are confident that your idea is solid and you've done your homework.

- You work with an accountant on a financial plan to mitigate losses, and you get help with marketing and building up the profile of your venture.

- You build a strong, trusted network of people within the restaurant industry and with farmers and local growers.

- You collaborate with chefs you admire. You try out new dishes, turn specials into menu favorites, and start to build a friendly group of regulars who frequent your restaurant.

And so on. Bottom line is you have a road map and you're following it to your destination, asking for help when you need it and persevering. But . . . let's say the restaurant struggled because of economic factors beyond your control and you decided you couldn't renew the lease. Is it all for nothing? No! You were bold and you aren't walking away empty-handed.

- You learned you could persevere under stress and work harder than you ever imagined.

- You learned how to become more patient with your staff and how to fire someone who wore you down, despite their talent.

- You understood that while it's not the outcome you set out to have, all is not lost. You can take your experience with you in a new direction and open a different kind of restaurant or a restaurant in a different area of town. Or perhaps you've realized a food truck is a better way to serve up your most popular menu items.

You grew. You were humbled. You got stronger. You are bolder.

Risk is riddled with negativity. It is defined as the possibility of loss or injury. Bold is bursting with positivity. It is being fearless and showing confidence. When you take a risk, there's a chance you will end up with less than when you started. When you make a bold move, worse comes to worst, you're right back where you started. More likely, you will have so much more. You believe that even if you fail, you can't lose.

Is it risky or bold to leave your job and start the business you've been tinkering with for a while? If you don't have a way to pay the rent and feed yourself (and the people who depend on you) before your business draws income, it's a risk. If you work on the business after work and on the weekends, it's a bold move.

Making a bold move in your career, in love, or in a creative endeavor doesn't guarantee everything will turn out as you hoped, but you will have accumulated some pretty cool dots. You'll have learned what worked and what didn't. You'll have built up your resilience to failure and heartbreak. You'll be ahead of the game. You'll have moved forward.

Pick a Start Date

Let's say you've mitigated the risks and are ready to start your bold journey. Now what? Do you just wake up the next day and get started? Is it better to start on a Monday? On the first day of the month? The first day of the year? Your birthday? The answer is: yes.

Katy Milkman, PhD, author of *How to Change: The Science of Getting from Where You Are to Where You Want to Be,* suggests choosing a monumental date to get started, which she has termed the "fresh start effect." That big date could be a birthday, the anniversary of when you started your first "real" job, January 1, exactly three months after graduation, etc. Milkman, a professor at Wharton who is an expert on behavioral change, has researched the impact of selecting a significant start date for a new endeavor. Her studies have shown that when we select a personally meaningful date that symbolizes the beginning of a new chapter in our lives, we're especially motivated to persevere until we get what we want.

That said, you shouldn't wait around too long for that "monumental" date to arrive. If you decide New Year's Day is calling to you, but it's February, don't wait for January 1 to roll around again unless you've got a really good, bold reason (i.e., that's part of your business plan, for instance, and you'll be using the next eleven months to work on your launch). Instead, look at the calendar and decide on a date—don't overthink it.

Mark your calendar with your start date—do it, write the words BOLD START right there! You are now creating a dividing line between the past and your bigger, better, bolder future.

You have a map, a direction, and a departure date. It's time to get going.

Principle #8

Be Obsessively Curious

WHEN YOU HAVE A RELATIVELY common name like mine, it's not unusual to receive emails intended for someone else with the same name. It's happened to me several times, and I usually write back to the sender to let them know. But several years ago, one case stood out. A man had emailed this "Jennifer Cohen" instead of his literary agent, also named "Jennifer Cohen." But it took me a minute before I understood what had happened.

I thought: *Is this someone I know? His name doesn't look familiar . . . Why is this guy sending me his manuscript? It looks like an important book. Does he want me to read it? Why would he want me to read his manuscript?* I was so confused!

Once I realized it was just another case of mistaken email identity, I decided to make the occasion an opportunity. This man was clearly a successful writer and author. There were probably a bunch of interesting things I could learn

133

from him. My insatiable-curiosity switch flipped on, and I decided that instead of my usual "wrong Jennifer Cohen" reply, I'd take action.

Manuscript Man's phone number was in his email signature, so I called him. When he picked up, I introduced myself as Jennifer Cohen, only not the Jennifer Cohen he was expecting to hear from. I explained that I'd received his manuscript by mistake and wanted to make sure it didn't get lost in the cyperspace Jennifer Cohen confusion.

I could tell by his voice how shocked he was that I had gone to the trouble of calling him to let him know. As he said, "Most people would just have deleted the email and gone on their merry way."

And most people who received a call like the one I made would have said "thank you" and gone on their merry way. But not Manuscript Man. My gesture sparked a philosophical discussion about human nature, why people do what they do . . . and forty-five minutes later, we were still chatting, and the more we chatted, the more curious about Manuscript Man I became.

Somewhere along the way of our long and winding conversation, I learned he was a *New York Times* best-selling author, a political commentator, and a writer for *Forbes* and several other prestigious media outlets. Now I was really curious about this guy. I wanted to know everything about him and his writing background!

How long have you been a professional writer? What kind of book did you write? Is it your first book? How many books have you written? What are they about? Did you always want to be a writer?

And then, finally, I asked him how he had become a writer for *Forbes*. I realized there was an opportunity here; maybe I could write an article for *Forbes*. I began spitballing article ideas off the top of my head, thinking to myself: *What's the worst that can happen? He hangs up on me? I never talk to him again? If he does blow me off, I am no worse off than I was an hour ago before I knew this dude even existed. And he seems to want to keep talking.*

"What do you think about a column on productivity?" I asked. "I can write a great piece on how executives can be their most productive." All the fundamentals of fitness—like energy, focus, discipline, and goal setting—are habits people can use to become more productive at work.

My new buddy hesitated and then said he liked the idea but wasn't sure it would be a great fit for the *Forbes* reader or that his editor would go for it. As if that was going to stop me.

"Well," I said, "there's only one way to find out! Let's ask!"

He hemmed and hawed a bit about making the introduction to his editor but finally agreed to it. Also, he knew I had his number and email address, and that I was not going to let this opportunity go! If he didn't act within the next day or two, I'd be following up. And indeed I had to, but Manuscript Man eventually connected me to his editor, John, who would be reaching out to me. And that took a few more follow-up emails on my part, but eventually John gave me a shot to write an article on optimizing productivity.

A few days later, my first piece was published on Forbes .com and quickly rose in popularity to become the number-one most read article on the site that same day. John allowed me to submit a second article, which led to another, which turned into my own column on leadership and productivity that lasted six years—and just like that, I became an expert on the topic.

The *Forbes* column gave me the opportunity to meet and talk with people I otherwise wouldn't have had the chance to connect with. I had been pigeonholed many times in my career—I was "just" a fitness expert, to some—but I had so much more to say. My curiosity in that phone call proved to be a game changer.

Let Curiosity Set Your Direction

My decision to seize the opportunity of an email mix-up and connect with a successful writer resulted in a defining moment in my career. Having the name *Forbes* behind me meant people took me more seriously as a businessperson and an expert on brand building and negotiating—not just the woman who could do lots of squats and lunges. My curiosity helped me break out of the box that others often put me in.

When I made that call that day, I leveraged several bold skills to get the results I wanted:

- I followed a direction, not a destination. I was totally open to where a call to a complete stranger would lead me.

- I believed in myself and my ability to deliver a product I sensed was desirable.

- I practiced bold habits, including asking for something that I wanted. I pushed aside self-doubt by also asking myself the big question: *What's the worst that can happen?*

- I was obsessively curious.

When you're obsessively curious and open, you can expand your bold reach wider and deeper—you won't ever settle for what's right in front of you. Numerous studies—including research from the University of California, Davis, Center for Neuroscience done with functional MRI technology—show that we learn best, and the most, when we're genuinely curious about the subject matter. Scientists describe a "vortex effect" in our brains, meaning that when we're curious about a particular topic, we not only absorb and retain that information but we also pull in peripheral knowledge once our brains are stimulated. In other words, if you walk into a situation curious about one thing, you may wind up walking away having learned about many things.

This phenomenon applies in everyday situations that can lead you along a bolder path. For instance, if you're curious about the person standing next to you at a networking event (or in the coffee shop), and you start asking a few questions, you are likely going to gain a lot of information that you may be able to put to very good use. I was genuinely intrigued by Manuscript Man and his writing career, and our lively conversation—where I asked lots of questions, as I always do—took me in a positive direction.

The next time you meet someone you find remotely interesting, get curious about them. You never know what you'll learn and where your questions may lead. Always be open to exploring how their answers can benefit your goals. If you see a slight opening, open it wider and see what's there for you to explore. Be ready to show how you can add value for this person, their customers, or their clients. Be clear about how hard you are ready to work for what you want. If you're not getting the response you want, or any response at all, try again. Keep at it. Persistence often pays off. Nurture your curiosity with bold moves like these:

Talk to Strangers

Never pass up an opportunity to meet new people. Next time you're at a dinner party or work event, don't sit next to friends or colleagues. Find a seat beside someone you don't know, introduce yourself politely, and start by asking open-ended questions. Look for the person who is alone nursing a cocktail and engage them in conversation. You don't have to have anything in common with them other than the fact that you're at the same event, but once you start getting curious, I bet you'll find reasons why this person appeared in your orbit.

One a Day

Try to meet one new person a day. It can be someone who sent an email to your address by mistake, the person sitting near you at your coworking space, or your kid's friend's parent you happen to be sitting next to at the soccer game. And get obsessively curious about who they are, what they do, why they do it, etc. Be genuine, be sincere, and be open to where their answers will take you.

Party Trick

Host a party where you ask each guest to bring someone you have never met, and whom your other guests likely won't know either. Pair off guests with someone they don't know. Each guest has five minutes to ask their partner questions while revealing nothing about themselves until they switch and the other one has five minutes to ask questions. When the ten minutes are up, each guest has one or two minutes to introduce their partner to all the party guests as if they've known them their whole lives.

My husband and I have hosted game nights at our house with different groups of friends—we like to encourage them to bring guests who are new to our circle, as it makes things more interesting! We play games like Pictionary as well as a game called "celebrity," where you break into teams and have to guess the name of a notable figure with clues and charades (you can find simple instructions online for this popular party game). These experiences are great icebreakers and loads of fun—low-pressure, low-stakes ways to boost curiosity and reap the benefits.

Go Down the Rabbit Hole

Curiosity isn't limited to meeting new people, of course. Is there a topic you've been thinking about for a while that really piques your interest? Indulge your curiosity and do a deep dive. (This is where you can give yourself permission to Google stuff to your heart's content.) You never know what you'll learn until you fire up your brain and let it roam free.

Curiosity will feed your boldness. Now let's look at a surprising quality that's also essential: naivete.

Principle #9

Naivete Is a Strength

IF CURIOSITY IS A GOOD way to open doors of opportunity, then naivete is a great trait to have when walking through those doors. You may be thinking that being naive is a negative when you're trying to move forward, but I discovered early on that this quality is a bold booster—a powerful foil to the "age and experience required" mentality that stops many of us from going after what we want.

I was a twentysomething and living in Toronto when Barbara Walters launched her now-famous daytime talk show, *The View*, featuring strong, opinionated women from different generations and backgrounds. I quickly became hooked on the show and tuned in every day, eager to see what subjects and controversies the five cohosts would dive into.

But as the first two seasons of *The View* wore on, I noticed that many of the daily "hot topics" panel discussions, as well as the celebrity and expert segments, weren't resonating with my twentysomething peers. And that's when I saw a gap in the market and an opportunity for a show like *The View*, specifically designed for women in their twenties. Even though I had no experience, I would be the one to fill that gap. I'd create my own Canadian daily talk show for women in their twenties and call it *Blah Blah Blah*.

I knew it was a good idea. A *genius* idea! How could anyone think otherwise? It would be such an easy sell. *The View* already had the successful format, so I would copy that, tweak the content of the show to appeal to women my age, and cast five women in their twenties as cohosts. I mean, how hard could it be?

Famous last words. It was, no doubt, a little naive of me to think I could pitch a show and that it would get picked up and air on national TV. I had no TV industry experience. I didn't have any contacts in the TV biz. And why did I assume anyone would take a call from some random girl with a TV show idea? Not that I asked myself these very rational questions—but, as you'll see, that turned out to be the right move.

When you have a crazy idea, you ask the friend who is crazy like you to join forces. My best friend Laura was an equally driven and ambitious go-getter, and if anyone was going to climb aboard the big, bold idea train with me, it was her.

Laura and I began calling every single Canadian TV show producer we could find. We called and called and called . . . We were incredibly tenacious about it. Finally, we got the head of a major production company to agree to meet with us. He liked the idea and gave us $1,500 to film a fifteen-minute demo—not a ton of cash to work with, even in Canada, where production was considerably less expensive than in the United States. We had no video camera, no lighting equipment, no sound equipment, no video-editing skills, no studio to film in . . . you get the picture. What we did have in spades was determination, and a brilliant idea for our demo! We'd drive to Montreal, Quebec, for the annual Just for Laughs comedy festival and interview the big-name North American comics and Hollywood stars expected to be performing and hobnobbing there for days.

It was the perfect plan, except we hadn't thought through our meager budget limitations. Between the gas money for the six-hour drive from Toronto to Montreal, food, and the two-night stay we booked at the hotel where many of the comics were staying, our budget was gone. We had nothing left for the all-access passes we needed to be allowed into Just for Laughs. Did that stop us? Of course not! We were determined to get into the show and film our interviews for the demo. All we needed were passes and a video camera.

The first challenge was getting that camera. Even if we *had* festival passes, we'd need a camera and mics to film our interviews. This one was easy, though maybe a bit, uh, sneaky. We bought an 8 mm camera and some mics at Best Buy, planning to use and return them. Then, we went to an art-supply store and found black cord that was an exact match for the Just for Laughs pass lanyards. We hung the black cord around our necks and tucked the ends under our shirts to make it seem like our passes were just innocently hidden under there. It worked! We boldly walked right past security and into the festival.

Once we were past the gates, we talked up everyone—managers, producers, agents, and the kind of big stars we were after to shoot for the demo. Laura and I interviewed loads of impressive people, doing our best to make it seem like we were a sophisticated crew with a show already on the air. But when we checked the tape, we immediately discovered that the first videos we filmed were choppy, the sound was awful, and the lighting was even worse. We were determined, but we were also realistic, and there was no way we'd get anywhere with a lousy-quality demo.

Fortunately, the venue was packed with seasoned TV people, and that's how we met an agreeable ABC cameraman who offered to film a few of our interviews. I got Howie Mandel for one! Fred Willard for another! *90210*'s Luke Perry!

Two women with no credentials or experience (not to mention official lanyards) got about two dozen comics and actors to agree to be interviewed for a show that didn't yet exist, shot by a veteran cameraman with his state-of-the-art equipment, for free. When Laura and I returned to Toronto after our bold escapade (and returned the camera to Best Buy, of course), I invested my own money to have the film professionally edited into a fifteen-minute daytime TV talk show demo that I had no doubt the big-time producer would love.

And he did! He was really impressed. But did *Blah Blah Blah* ever make it on the air? No. The decision was obviously out of my control. What *was* in my control was the journey I took to do everything I could to get the show as far as I could get it to go. My bold move wasn't a failure; I learned a ton about production that I'd put to use later in my career.

Though the doors closed on the *Blah Blah Blah* TV show, a new opportunity opened up. Several Hollywood agents had been at Just for Laughs and noticed my bold go-getter moves. They liked my hustle and thought I'd make a good agent or manager. I was offered a slot in a coveted training program at 3 Arts Entertainment, the talent-management agency and TV/film production company in Los Angeles.

So I packed up and moved to LA—and lasted, approximately, ten days on the job. I watched as assistants got eaten alive by celebrity clients for ordering the wrong flowers, chewed up for not picking up someone's dry cleaning, and spit out for not finding a celebrity's lost dog. (Seriously, a young trainee was dispatched to the Hollywood Hills to track down a famous person's missing dog—"And don't bother coming back to the office until you find that damn dog!" The poor guy never came back. He could still be out there looking for that damn dog.)

Maybe I was too much of a "nice Canadian," but taking crap all day wasn't for me. Being bold doesn't mean you have to let people treat you like dirt, and I realized that I didn't want to chase a career as a talent agent. My boss, actually, was not a bad guy at all—and when I came in to give notice he was surprised I'd lasted ten days! Fortunately, through someone else I met at the agency, I was offered a job at Immortal Records, a division of Sony Music, which laid the groundwork for my next bold moves.

I tapped into many bold Principles during this experience: believing in my idea, following a direction and not a destination, being obsessively curious (I love asking people questions!), and more. But what really worked for me in this instance was my naivete. It got me to Los Angeles and set me up for the rest of my career. Had I known what it would take to get that demo done, I might have backed down. Had I had years of production experience behind me, I might have been stuck in analysis paralysis, overthinking all the ways to perfect the demo I'd never finish.

And there's another big lesson here: it's just as important to find out what you *don't* want as it is to know what you do want. Trying lots of things can help you fine-tune your direction.

The Less You Know, the Freer You Are

The power of naivete is that, while you may lack experience and knowledge, you tend to take chances because you don't know any better, and you can see ways around roadblocks others can't see because they know too much. They have heard "no" and "you can't do that" and "that's not the way it's done" and "you don't have enough experience" so many times that they believe it's just the way things are. When you're held captive by rules and guidelines and boundaries, it's easy to become jaded, rigid, fearful, and ready to settle for whatever you get. But when you're naive, you don't even *know* that there are rules and guidelines and boundaries— which makes all of them easier to break!

Lack of experience is precisely what drives bold people to try harder and take bigger chances to pursue their goals. Here are some pointers for leaning into what you *don't* know.

Don't Act Your Age

I had the double advantage of being young *and* naive when I was trying to pitch my talk show idea. But you don't have to be in your twenties to practice the art of naivete. It's not age that limits us; it's our mindset. The older we get, the more we know, and certainly that can have its advantages. But at the same time, the older we get, the more we allow limiting ideas of what we can and cannot do decide our destiny for us.

Think of all the things you don't do—including hitting the reset button on a career or relationship—because you tell yourself you're too old. Imagine all the things you could do if you could forget about the year you were born. You are never too old to be bold, and you're never too experienced to let naivete work for you.

Sir Richard Branson, founder of the Virgin Group, has embraced naivete in every decade of his phenomenally successful life, opening his first record store at age twenty with barely any knowledge about the retail business. Two years later, he launched the Virgin Records music label. As he got older, Branson still used naivete to power his bold moves. In his thirties, when his flight to meet his future wife was canceled, he decided he could do a better job at running an airline himself, though he had no experience in the industry. "I chartered a plane, borrowed a blackboard, and wrote 'Virgin Airlines' on the top of the blackboard, '$39 one way to BVI' [British Virgin Islands]," Branson said on the CNBC podcast *The Brave Ones*. He says he filled up his first flight—and then he called up Boeing and cajoled them into selling him some used 747s. They hesitated given his naivete, but, eventually, Virgin Atlantic airlines wound up buying a lot of planes from Boeing.

What followed were bold moves roughly every decade of his life—moves that some might call naive. They were anything but . . .

- In his forties, he got into the telecom business with Virgin Mobile and started a railway.

- In his fifties, he decided commercial spaceflights would become a reality and founded Virgin Galactic.

- In his sixties, he worked with the United Kingdom's National Health Service to provide subsidized health care through the Virgin Care chain of clinics.

And while Branson may have been naive to think that he could take a rocket into space in 2004 when he started Virgin Galactic, in July 2021, just days shy of his seventy-first birthday, Sir Richard Branson spent fifteen minutes flying in space aboard the Virgin Galactic Unity 22 space plane.

Branson has credited his naivete and inexperience for his success as an entrepreneur. "Don't worry about being called naive," he has famously said. "My naivete has made me successful."

Be Guided by What You Want, Not by What You Know

Jewel, the singer-songwriter who has sold thirty million records worldwide, was nineteen and homeless, singing in West Coast coffeehouses, when she was scouted by an executive from Atlantic Records. Very quickly, they offered her a million-dollar record deal.

Anyone trying to break into the industry would have jumped on it, and fast. A record-label executive discovers a talented artist, invites them into their big, fancy office, offers them more money than they ever dreamed of, asks them to sign a contract, and the rest would be music-legend history, right? If you know how the music industry works, you know that most contracts give the labels loads of creative control and can turn a fairy-tale ending into a nightmare for some artists. That is, if you know how the music industry works.

But Jewel didn't. And that was her strength.

Jewel didn't take what was offered as pro forma. She went to the library and did her research. She learned that the deal she was being offered wasn't a guaranteed payment, but an advance. And if her records didn't sell enough to compensate for the advance, she'd be responsible for paying the balance back to the label. She'd also likely be dropped by the label, leaving her homeless once again and unable to pay back her debt. And most important to Jewel, she learned that once she signed with the label, they'd tell her what kind of music to write and how to perform it. As a folk singer during the height of the 1990s grunge era, Jewel imagined she'd be directed to write music that wasn't her style and she'd lose the strong fan base she'd already grown organically through her small-venue performances.

What Jewel did know was what she wanted: to be true to herself and her music. She chose that over being rich and famous, as the record execs were promising her. Jewel turned down the million-dollar record deal and instead negotiated for a larger piece of the back end than is normally agreed to and a small stipend to pay her rent and other essentials.

This deal structure also meant that the record label was more willing to let her first album find its fans as it found its way up the charts. Her first hit, "Who Will Save Your Soul," was released in 1995 and made it to number eleven on the *Billboard* Hot 100. It was the first song she'd ever written, when she was sixteen and homeless.

Jewel's bold move may seem very savvy now, but it was what she didn't know about the music industry that led her to seeing a better deal than what was standard at the time. She had the freedom to write and perform the music she wanted to, while earning much more than she would have with a traditional record deal.

Don't Know How? Learn As You Go

At age fourteen, Aidan Bryant was so inspired by watching musical artist Pink's aerial acrobatics performances on You-Tube that—despite his total lack of experience—he decided he wanted to try aerial acrobatics too. Aidan knew his family couldn't afford gymnastics lessons or any formal training in this very specialized area, but that didn't stop him. He watched as much Pink as he could find, then studied other aerial gymnastics routines on YouTube until he was ready to give it a shot. He tied one of his grandmother's bedsheets to a tree and began practicing what he had learned. Instead of saying, "No, you can't actually learn how to do aerial gymnastics by watching YouTube videos," Aidan's family encouraged him and found creative ways to help him practice as he tackled more and more challenging moves.

Two years later, the completely self-taught sixteen-year-old was performing aerial gymnastics for judges on NBC's *America's Got Talent*. He impressed all four judges and moved up to the next round, beating the competition week after week, until coming in second place overall in the finale. (In my opinion, Aidan should have won!)

Aidan got as far as he did because of his tenacious desire. He didn't let inexperience get in the way. He didn't let a lack of formal training stop him. He was guided by what he wanted, and he learned how to get it as he flew to the top, literally. You can watch Pink on YouTube, but if you really want inspiration from someone who tuned out the "no" and listened to the "yes," then watch Aidan on YouTube.

Never let what you don't know stop you from chasing what you want. Think of what you don't know as a strength. You will try harder. You will try new ideas. You will try new directions. You will seek out instruction where you can get it. You will try *anything*! And like Aidan, you will fly high.

Knowledge Is Power—but So Is Naivete

It's wise to be prepared, to do your homework, and to have your road map ready. (And it is possible for someone to take advantage of you if you're *too* naive. But bold skills like having direction and curiosity will always tip the balance back in your favor.) That said, if you're still hesitating to take a bold leap because you feel like you don't know *everything*, just remember that your lack of knowledge can be your bold advantage. If you think you know it all, you'll be woefully unprepared when someone or something throws a wrench in your plans. If you're willing to be the opposite of the smartest guy in the room, you'll be more open to learning, to problem-solving with new solutions, and to chasing what you want.

Exercise your naivete. Is there something you've always wanted to try, but have little or no knowledge of how to do? Go fly-fishing if you've never done it. Learn French. Get a blank canvas, some paints, and make some art. Take a Bollywood dance class, or a tennis lesson. Write and submit an opinion piece to your local paper. It's not about the outcome; it's about practicing feeling uncomfortable with not knowing all the answers, doing it anyway, and seeing where it leads you. My bet is that it takes you further down your own bold road.

Principle #10

Mediocrity Is a Superpower

I LIKE TO PRAISE A quality that may surprise you, as it isn't an attribute you might associate with successful people: mediocrity.

From a young age, we're told to be "the best"—the smartest, the fastest, the funniest, the prettiest, the winningest. But, practically speaking, most people will never fall into the "best" category—nor are they the "worst." Most of us are right in the middle. I sure was. I was mediocre, which some people consider to be less than average.

But mediocrity, despite its negative connotation, has real value. In fact, I believe it's a superpower, and that it can push you to achieve. Mediocrity compels us to compensate for weaknesses in one area by developing our other strengths, gifts we've had all along but may have overlooked. Mediocrity enables us to think beyond our expectations of ourselves and plan strategically to make up for weaknesses by leaning on our strengths to get what we want. Keep the following points in mind as you ponder this Principle.

It's OK to Be OK

Have you ever strained your back or hurt a knee? When your body is weak on one side, it naturally recruits the muscles on the uninjured side to compensate for weakness, which allows you to keep going. But balancing strength and weakness is not just a physical phenomenon—it can apply to personal traits and skills as well. It's impossible to be "the best" at everything, but you can get pretty far being OK at lots of things, and you can get really far if you look for ways to compensate for what you're bad at.

I'm proof that mediocrity can become an asset. You already know how I made up for my "average" academic standing by becoming resourceful, determined, and independent outside of the classroom. That grit, the result of my "average" status, has served me well for decades. Mediocrity made me bold, and my boldness has enriched my life. A rich life means never settling for a good enough life. And yet, time and time again, I encounter dissatisfied people who've settled into their own mediocrity without seeing all the ways it can actually take them to new heights.

"MEH" VERSUS "EH"

Just to clarify, embracing mediocrity and settling for good enough are two separate concepts.

If you're mediocre, average, or just OK at something—like cold-calling to further your business idea or setting aside money in your 401(k) or water skiing or speaking up to tell your partner what you want—that's very different from not doing it at all. If you're settling for good enough, or you've stopped trying to improve altogether, you're giving up. If you're OK or even if you kind of suck at the activity in question but you're doing it anyway, you're still flexing your bold muscles. You can be mediocre at poker—meaning that you may not win every hand—but at least you're in the game. And the more you keep playing, chances are high the better you'll get.

You Don't Have to Be the Best, but You Can Still Get What You Want

Some people make the mistake of thinking that they don't deserve to get what they want because it's reserved for those who are *the best*, who have the most talent, experience, strength, brains, beauty, and so on. Those traits do matter if you're competing in the Tour de France, for Miss Universe, or on *Jeopardy!*, I suppose, but unless you're chasing a goal where quantifiable results are the sole deciding factor, like an Olympic time trial, what is stopping you?

Break out of your self-determined limitations and "choose yourself," as author and entrepreneur James Altucher said on my podcast. You can either think to yourself: *I'm really so mediocre at this! I can barely do it. I have a weakness, so I should give this up.* Or you can decide you're worthy of more and think: *I have a weakness, but I won't let it stop me from getting what I want. I'll find a way.*

It's easy to use "but I'm not the best" as an excuse to be complacent and sit things out, or you can use mediocrity and weakness as catalysts for change. Bold is about taking a shot and then taking another shot when you don't succeed. Ask yourself about opportunities you didn't take, or even see in front of you until it was too late, because you let "but I'm not the best" rule your mindset. Ask yourself about an opportunity in front of you *right now*. Why haven't you chosen to pursue it? Is it because you're waiting to become the best? My advice is, don't wait! Instead, ask yourself this: How can you leverage your existing strengths, or draw on other people's strengths, to go after what you want?

Use What You've Got to Get What You Want

Understanding your strengths is as important as knowing your weaknesses. And focusing on our strengths instead of weaknesses has the power to change our mindset. Researchers have found that people find it much easier to make a list of weaknesses they want to improve upon than a list of the strengths they want to build on. We already have great things going for us, and yet when it comes to self-improvement, we're often focused on fixing our weaknesses, and that proves to be a bit of a downer if we fail (trying and failing to lose weight is a good example). On the other hand, identifying our strengths and putting them to work can lead to a more positive mindset. In one so-called positive intervention program, participants identified their top five strengths and then were challenged to use them in new ways. After six weeks, they were happier and less depressed about their perceived weaknesses.

If you can't move forward because you're stuck on the fact that you're so-so, just OK, mediocre, average, not the best, or bad at something, it's time to shift into a bolder gear. Try this exercise, which will set you up for the next Principle, Bundle Your Bold.

Make a list of your strengths, including character traits like kindness, humor, leadership, and integrity. List your professional strengths like being a good manager or networker. You may even want to ask a friend, family member, or coworker to offer their insights. Then, do your own positive intervention program: consider ways you can improve on some of these strengths, one week at a time.

For instance, do you have a good sense of humor? Then share your strength. Post a cartoon or tell a colleague a funny story, just to get a smile and lift their spirits. Are you organized? Share your strength with someone who could use your help, like a tween who can't ever find anything in her backpack, or an elderly relative whose messy desk is causing him to misplace important financial documents. Are you a good baker? Share your strength and surprise your work mates with a fresh batch of lemon bars.

While some of these things may seem just like pay-it-forward good deeds (and they are), they're also serving another purpose: they're ways for you to celebrate your strengths, making you more confident and helping you sharpen skills you already have.

Think of your strengths as muscles you should build and maintain with exercise, to compensate for weaker muscles. A 2015 Gallup analysis found that "people who use their strengths every day are three times more likely to report having an excellent quality of life [and] six times more likely to be engaged at work." So there's another payoff here too: using your strengths regularly is good for your overall well-being.

Principle #11

Bundle Your Bold

WHEN I JOINED IMMORTAL RECORDS after I left 3 Arts, I worked in marketing, launching and promoting music artists. It was a good gig, and we had loads of fun.

That is, until the death of the "album." iTunes redefined the way people purchased music and the way all digital media is consumed. Instead of people buying full albums, they were able to buy one song at a time, which seriously cut into profits. On top of that, the practice of illegal downloading was rampant. It started with hackers, but it became a mainstream way of accessing the latest in pop music—and at a great cost.

Services like iTunes and Napster shook the traditional recording industry to the core, and almost overnight, the old ways of doing business were no longer relevant. As record sales plummeted and dot-coms boomed, digital marketing became the new standard. Up to that point, I'd loved my job—I had interesting work at a great salary, an office filled with cool people (not to mention a view of the beach), and I could ride my bike to work. It was heaven. And it was history, for me at least. I had no passion for digital marketing campaigns, and I knew it was time to move on.

I didn't want to sit in another office in front of a computer screen, and while I didn't know exactly what I wanted to do next, I knew that I loved exercise and fitness—it had changed my brain. With that bit of direction, and given that I needed to make some money, I decided to become a certified personal trainer and started considering my long-term options. I had come to LA armed with my homegrown bold skills, but also with a bachelor's degree in psychology and a master's degree in sports marketing. I'd worked for the Toronto Raptors during the first year of the franchise, for the sports-management agency IMG, and for BMG Music.

My first two clients were the parents of a friend who threw me a bone until I figured out my next move. And that's when I landed on an idea that would combine my knowledge and skills from my previous jobs in marketing with my love of fitness. Because of lagging album sales, the music industry was putting even more emphasis on getting its biggest talent out on tour. More than ever, concert performances and music videos were vital to an artist's success (and the label's), but the top talent wasn't necessarily in top shape to handle the strenuous requirements of nonstop touring, making videos, and performing live, night after night.

I saw an empty niche that I was perfectly suited to fill. I decided to pitch myself to one of my former contacts in the music business as a fitness trainer to the talent. The singers and musicians would need to be trained to get in shape and improve their stamina to keep up with the rigors of touring. Not only would I help them get and stay in shape physically, but I'd be helping them to be mentally prepared as well.

I wrote out a list of all the things I had going for me, and the more I jotted down, the more confident I was that I had a solid-gold idea.

- ✓ Fitness training certification? Check.

- ✓ Ability to demonstrate how regular workouts would also improve mindset? Check.

- ✓ Passion for music? Check.

- ✓ Deep knowledge of the music industry? Check.

- ✓ Deeper knowledge of the music label? Check.

- ✓ Understanding of marketing budgets? Check.

- ✓ Understanding of the energy and focus touring requires of the talent? Check.

- ✓ Capacity to deal with the whims of celebrity talent? Check.

- ✓ Good relationships at the label? Check.

The list went on and on. *Check. Check. Check.*

I put my pitch together and set up a meeting to present my fresh idea: label trainer, the personal trainer for the label's roster of talent. They loved it!

I was immediately set up to train major talent, including Britney Spears, Christina Aguilera, Mickey Guyton, Christina Milian, and many more, getting them in top form and helping them stay fit for their demanding live performances, music videos, and touring schedules. My venture took off! Label training was so popular that I took the concept to a second record label, and then a third.

There was, of course, only so much training I could personally do, so I hired a few trainers to work with me and expanded my business. It was incredibly exciting and satisfying to forge my own path, create my own job, and then be able to offer jobs to talented trainers. I did all this by doing something you're about to learn: Principle #11, Bundle Your Bold.

Always remember: you're bolder—and more skilled—than you think. As we just discussed in Principle #10, focus on your strengths, and you have plenty. No matter how you may need to pivot to chase what you want, you're never starting from scratch. Somewhere in your journey, you've collected those dots of experience—which translate to micro skills *and* macro skills that can benefit your next career move, or whatever personal goal you may have your eye on. By bundling together select skills you already possess, you'll find that you have a head start on getting what you want.

When it comes to making a bold career switch, in particular, I always give this advice to people who feel their options are limited because of their past work experience or a specific degree: Think outside the resumé. Your bundle of skills doesn't have to be solely based on formal education or career experience. It also includes the skills you've picked up along the way, even if you don't see right now how they factor into your next move, and even if you're not "the best" at executing them; you still have some know-how. (Connect those dots. Remember Steve Jobs and his calligraphy class? You just never know.)

Bundling your bold is a way to gather your education, career experience, talents and skills, and networks and package them into a powerhouse of complementary skills. Let's tackle each of these categories separately.

Education

Education is not just about a formal degree or certification. It's about all the ways you were educated, in and out of school, and it also includes things you learned on your own. If you majored in finance and you want to launch an investing app but need to wow some investors, maybe it's the acting classes you took on the side that will set you apart. Consider how that stage experience could help in talking up your exciting idea when you do your big pitches. Or informal education may come from being a voracious reader. I began reading books by entrepreneurs about how they built their businesses when I was in grade school. I also loved reading autobiographies of people I was fascinated with. That reading material wasn't on any class syllabus—it just intrigued me. What "extras" have you learned that might fill out your bundle?

(Obviously, formal education is essential if you want to pivot into some fields. For example, you can't just switch from teaching piano to practicing law and skip the law school part. But think about how you can bundle your bold when you're completing your law school applications.)

Career Experience

If you are looking to pivot from one industry to another, or even if you're looking to leap into a related field, try bundling your bold job experiences, even if they seem unrelated. I bundled my bold skills when I went from working at the label to coming back as a label trainer. And then I did it again, making a leap into a whole new industry. Sometimes your transferable skills are not obvious; always be on the lookout for what you can take from one job or career to another.

My label training business was really working, but I was burning out, physically and mentally. I was working out with my clients, working out on my own, running the business, managing staff, and one day I just realized I'd had enough.

I knew I needed to pivot, and I put the word out to a select few friends in my network. The record label executive who'd first hired me became a dear friend and knew I was in need of a change, so he referred me to Andrew Gilman, who was running a very successful and highly regarded media-training company with offices in Washington, DC, New York, and LA. The DC office focused mostly on politics, the New York office handled primarily finance, and the West Coast branch would focus on entertainment and biotech (lots of biotech). I was skeptical that it would be a good fit, but my friend convinced me to at least have coffee with Andrew.

First off, at least on a resumé, I was not qualified for the job. I had never media trained anyone, so I'd have to learn a new skill, and fast. And second, it sounded very corporate, and I am not a corporate type. I was never going to wear a suit to work, nor would I ever act buttoned-up. That aspect of it was simply not me, but . . . I was really intrigued, and I was ready for a change. I decided that if Andrew was cool with my style, I'd take the leap. *After all*, I thought, asking myself that magic question, *what is the worst that could happen?*

Andrew had a similar thought. He knew media training wasn't my wheelhouse, but he learned how I had built and grown my specialty fitness business out of nothing. Remember, "label trainer" wasn't even a job when I'd pitched it to my former boss at Immortal. Andrew liked that, since it meant he could get me an office and a desk and I'd figure it out from there. He also suspected I'd be a great salesperson (which turned out to be true). Andrew offered me the job, "no jacket required."

It was a hard pivot, and I had a lot to learn. I was open-minded. I learned from my mistakes and from my new mentor, Andrew. I worked with clients like eBay, Activision, and Warner Bros., and eventually my network expanded into biotech and finance. Bundling my bold resulted in a big life change that was precisely the move I needed at the time.

Talents and Skills

I think of talents as the things we are "naturally" good at—like singing, dancing, running fast, or telling jokes—in other words, not classic job skills (unless you're a professional entertainer, athlete, or comedian). Skills are things we learn through instruction and practice: a foreign language, computer programming, etc. We almost always remember to put skills down on our resumé or in job applications, but we may not automatically think of talents as being important in the same way, particularly if we've never applied our talents for career purposes. However, both should be included in your bundle of bold. If you naturally have artistic talent, or a way with words, or have always been comfortable with tech stuff, add those as options to choose from in your bundle. For example, you can use your art skills to design your company logo for your tutoring business. You can use your writing talents to produce a newsletter to send to clients. You can use your tech savvy to build your own digital platform and set up online payment options.

Networks

I used my network to bundle my bold and jump from one field to another. Friends, family, current and former coworkers, former classmates, community members, gym buddies, and so on are all within your network. When it comes to making bold moves that require an introduction to a new contact, spread a wide net and reach beyond your usual circle. Go through your contacts and social media friends, using LinkedIn connections and other platforms to jog your memory. Then think about who *they* might know. You may have forgotten that your cousin Lucy is married to a guy who works in the industry you want to break into, or you may notice that your former client has started a new business in a related field. Get familiar with what your acquaintances (and their acquaintances) are doing. Your next bold move could simply be getting back in touch.

What's in Your Bundle?

By bundling my bold, I created a new kind of job for myself and found success, and not just once. I pivoted from the record business to fitness, then back to the label as a fitness trainer. Then I bundled my bold again when I entered the media-training business. I did it again when I returned to the fitness industry with different goals in mind, and I've never stopped. If I have an idea I want to develop, I consider how I can bundle my bold to get what I want.

Now it's your turn. What do you have to offer? What are your transferable skills? What are your assets and strengths? Start making your own list as you focus on what you do know instead of what you don't. And think about personal skills as much as professional ones.

Do you have a sport or hobby you practice regularly that you can apply to your pursuit? Can you take your expert sewing know-how and marketing skills up a notch and start designing and selling those handmade baby clothes everyone loves? Are you a salesperson and a rock-climbing enthusiast who can coach business executives to reach new heights? What about bundling your party-planning skills with your ability to negotiate deals? Did you coach the Little League team to victory, even though you barely knew the rules of the game? That speaks to your ability to learn new skills quickly and think on your feet. Some or none of these examples may resonate with you, but the point is this: you may have complementary skills from different areas of your life that can get you to where you want to be.

Write down everything you can think of—this is not the time to be modest about what you're good at. Then be bold and enlist friends, colleagues, and loved ones to add to the list, because we tend to overlook skills we take for granted. They may remind you that you're a great connector, always linking friends together for social events and career networking. Or perhaps they'll praise your leadership ability when you led a parent group at your kid's school, or your problem-solving skills when you figured out how your community could recycle items more efficiently.

Keep adding to your bundle, practicing the skills you already have as you add new ones, and watch it grow over time into something bigger, better, and bolder.

Principle #12

Fix It, Farm It Out, Forget It

LONG BEFORE THE PANDEMIC MADE working out at home or outdoors the only way to keep fit when gyms and fitness studios were closed, I set out to design an easy, simple solution to help people integrate fitness and healthy living into their everyday life without having to get to the gym or own fancy equipment. My philosophy has always been to eliminate all excuses and make getting healthy simple and easy. As a working mom, especially when my kids were babies, even I, a fitness expert, found reasons to skip a workout. But excuses are a dime a dozen and each time I cashed one in, I felt worse for it. Working out gives us all more energy, not less. Even a quick ten- or fifteen-minute HIIT routine is enough to prime us for the day when we're short on time. Plus, the mood enhancers that come from a workout can last the entire day.

I knew from my own experience that by removing barriers and replacing them with easy, simple solutions for workouts, diet, and nutrition, I could help anyone get the body and mindset they needed to get through the day—and life! That's when I had the idea for No Gym Required, a fitness brand that offered products and services based on my "anytime, anywhere, no excuses" philosophy. In 2009, I released my first book, *No Gym Required: Unleash Your Inner Rock Star*, to give readers simple solutions to be healthier and more fit without going to the gym, featuring exercises you could do anywhere with minimal equipment.

Then I had an even bolder idea. What if you could take the "gym" with you wherever you went? My product was the NGR (as in, No Gym Required) shoe line. The concept was based on a removable weighted midsole. When you wore the sneaker with the special midsole, you burned up to 50 percent more calories when you walked because of the added resistance. When you wore it with a regular midsole, it was an everyday sneaker. NGR was the first company to design weighted shoes for fitness and fashion.

It was a bold move to decide to enter the shoe business with no experience under my belt. And it was also pretty bold to do it with a product that was entirely new to the market. The challenge with being the first, however, is *that you're the first*. It took a while, but I finally found a company in Korea that made a midsole like the one I wanted for my shoe.

The design, marketing, promotion, and sales of NGR shoes were tasks I felt comfortable attempting. In fact, I loved that part of the journey. However, it quickly became apparent that manufacturing issues, operations challenges, and financial spreadsheets were not my core competencies. I had no idea how to solve the problems that were coming at me. I knew that if I didn't find a solution, and if I stalled over what to do, I'd be losing time, money, and opportunities . . . not to mention, I'd likely lose the business.

Just as I thought NGR shoes were doomed, I remembered that I had a contact at a company I'd done some work with, a guy I really got along with well named Laurence Isaac. He was super entrepreneurial in his thinking. Laurence liked the NGR concept and decided to quit his job to come on board to handle operations and finance. I would oversee the rest. And just like that we became business partners, fifty-fifty. (Laurence was pretty bold to take this flier—and he still is!)

We had no money and needed massive amounts of it to stand out and shine among the big players in the sneaker category. I'm talking $50 million to $100 million budgets for marketing and advertising campaigns! We needed to find creative ways to get our product out there. I would spend most of my time and energy on sales, marketing, and communications—all of which I was good at, as these were my strengths. I was knocking on the doors of every connection I had to help me spread the word, calling and pitching every writer I found in the magazines I pored over. I spent a lot on "gifting" the shoes to people who I hoped would help me promote them. (I learned fast that that can be very costly—be careful not to give away too much if you're launching a new product!)

My shoes miraculously ended up on some famous feet. Courteney Cox wore them, as did Denise Richards. Stars saw them being worn by other stars and tastemakers, and I was able to place photos of celebs wearing NGR shoes in magazines like *Us Weekly*, *Life & Style*, *In Touch*, and other hot publications—remember, this was before influencers, Instagram, and TikTok! We marketed the shoes the old-fashioned way—by hoping someone famous would be photographed wearing them, and praying that the photo would be published.

The company and the shoes were starting to hit their stride. NGR shoes were getting buzz, and now we were selling so many pairs that some of the major shoe companies were taking note. However, we had one huge problem! The weighted insoles added significant weight to the shipments, which added to the already high freight costs. The shoes that were being manufactured and shipped from Korea were costing a fortune, and we couldn't get the prices down enough unless we ordered enormous quantities. It was becoming an operational nightmare. Meanwhile, our customers wouldn't pay us until shipments arrived, plus sixty days.

Had it just been me at the helm, I may have gone down with the shipping-costs problem then and there. I wouldn't have known all the ins and outs of finance and securing a loan that would help us keep the shipments on schedule and our customers satisfied. Laurence was handling all this, doing an excellent job as I held up my end of the entrepreneurial bargain, continuing to market and promote our product using all the skills in my bundle of bold and then some. Together, Laurence and I were a winning team with a fantastic first-to-market product. Had I hesitated to acknowledge my weaknesses and find a way to compensate for them, I would not have been able to focus my time and energy on my strengths. And that is a lesson you're about to learn for yourself with Principle #12.

The 3Fs Method

When we get stuck in place and can't follow through on our bold moves, it's because we're paralyzed by our deficits and insecurities. But the 3Fs Method enables us to compartmentalize those tasks that are getting in the way, allowing for the mental space to focus on the things that we're good at and the problems that are holding us back. Use the 3Fs to optimize your strengths and compensate for your weaknesses, which is what I did when I got my shoe company up and running.

Here's how it works. You've been laid off from your sales job at Big Box Store, Inc., and decide that now's the time to make a bold move and start the homemade cookie business you've been dreaming about for years. Friends, family, and coworkers love your cookies and have always encouraged you to sell them. You've thought it through and have lots of ideas for making your cookie business stand out, as well as a business plan for slow but steady growth.

You decide it's time, and with the layoff you have a good reason to hit the reset button on your work life. You believe in yourself and your idea, and you've got a road map. So you start your journey.

You open an Instagram account for your business—let's call it Boldie's Cookies. You buy the ingredients for your most popular cookies and begin by baking for friends and family for birthdays, anniversaries, and other special occasions. In return for free treats, you ask them to post the cookies on Instagram, tagging your account. Soon you're getting local orders here and there and you're officially in business. (And your friends and relatives also start paying you!) The pace is steady and manageable for a one-person operation.

And then, things speed up overnight. A mom influencer in another state who knows someone who knows someone who went to a kid's party where your cookies were a big hit shares your mini masterpieces in her Instagram story. The thing is, she has more than five hundred thousand Instagram followers, and now your DMs are blowing up with orders. Weeks after deciding to start Boldie's Cookies, you are overwhelmed with requests from moms around the country asking how they can order your cookies for *their* kid's party. And the backlog gets worse when a local food writer gets wind of your business and publishes a piece on the new baker in town. Now it's not just moms on Instagram who want Boldie's Cookies!

Most small-business owners would be celebrating this success, but you are stressing out. You don't just have to produce the product, but now you also have to carefully pack these fragile items for overnight shipping, keep track of who ordered how many of which type of cookies and for when, and get them shipped. You don't have a real logo, enough packaging materials, professional labels, a website that takes credit cards, a person to help you, or a big enough oven!

Now's the time to make decisions with the 3Fs Method so you can keep Boldie's Cookies from crumbling. Do you fix it? Can you farm it out? Or should you forget it?

Fix It

Fix it yourself when it can't be done by anyone else. Fix it yourself if it's your strength and you love doing the task (and you have time). I did this when I took on all the marketing and promotion tasks for NGR. Fix it yourself even if you're not great at it but you want to do it; you'll get better over time, and the pleasure you get will give you a bold rush. And fix it yourself even if you dislike doing the task but it must be done to save the day—until you can farm it out (coming up next).

179

- You are asked to come up with a signature cookie for a big-time VIP event, but the due date conflicts with a few other things. But, this is a major order that could transform your business, so it's worth rearranging your other commitments to make it happen. Fix it.

- The chips for your trademark chocolate chip cookies are expensive, but you don't want to compromise the taste with a switch to cheaper chocolate and harm your brand. You don't consider yourself to be a negotiating whiz, but you like talking to new people and this is something you have to do yourself. You visit the gourmet grocer who stocks the chips (armed with lots of tasty samples), finding common ground when you point out that you're also an independent business trying to make a go of it. You walk away with a deal to buy the chips in bulk in exchange for a discount. Bold move—you fixed it!

Farm It Out

Farm it out when a task is essential to your goals but you don't have to do it yourself. You can't be the expert on everything. It's better to do a handful of tasks well than to do a bunch of stuff poorly. Even worse, if you don't delegate tasks to experts who can help, you might run your bold dream into the ground. That almost happened to me, until I brought

Laurence in to help me with NGR and work his magic with spreadsheets and operations. If you have to spend money to bring in an expert, it's generally worth it if the future of your business is on the line.

- You're a baker, not a graphic designer. Boldie's Cookies are tiny works of art, but design a logo? Not your thing. Graphics for your packaging? Not your thing. Your teenage niece who is brilliant at that stuff and is thinking of making it her career? It's her thing. Farm it out by turning the design work over to your niece (who will be thrilled to be hired).

- You need a more sophisticated website to track orders, with links and features to showcase your product better. You've heard about these free or cheap plug-and-play websites, where you just have to drag this here and that there and, voilà, you have an online store! But after logging hours at your laptop trying to crack the code, your website looks worse than what you had before. Quit messing around and farm it out to a freelancer platform like 99designs or Fiverr, or ask around and hire a pro in your area.

- Don't be afraid to really farm it out and bring in a co-owner or partner down the road, depending on your business. For me, finance, supply chain, and general business operations weren't my expertise, but bringing in Laurence as a partner allowed me to focus on the things I did best.

Forget It

This is the third and final F—and let's just say "forget it" is a polite twist on the other f-word that comes to mind when I find myself confronted with a time-wasting, nonessential task or a negative thought that's getting in the way of my next bold move. When making a bold move to get the life we want, sometimes the best thing to do is just let go.

- A perfectly clean house? Devote a few minutes a day to the minimal tasks and then forget it. No one is judging your performance based on whether you unloaded the dishwasher.

- A tiny issue like shipping labels that are a shade darker than you expected? As long as the address is correct and the labels are readable, no one will notice but you. Forget it. At NGR, I agonized over a minor design detail that had no bearing on the quality of the product or sales. I eventually forgot it.

- Responding to every single comment or like on social media? That's an endless task. Forget it (or farm

182

it out—customer feedback and engagement is important, but don't get stuck on the small stuff).

Let go of things that aren't directly related to your goals. You don't need distractions, especially if you're at a make-or-break point. You can circle back to cleaning your house or ordering new labels later. No one important will judge you on the small stuff—but if you lose track of the bigger goal, you'll lose your direction.

The Fourth F: Focus

The 3Fs are especially useful if you're trying to launch your own business. But you can certainly use them if you're trying to improve your performance at work and jump to the next level, or you can even apply them outside of work. Use the 3Fs to fix the things you want to change about yourself. Maybe it's that you'd like to have a healthier lifestyle or get serious with your partner. Farm out the stuff that's bugging you (hire someone to clean your house or ask your family to pitch in more). And forget the things you can't easily change but that you can eventually accept (I don't love my nose, but I choose to leave it the way it is—and forget it). Think of the 3Fs Method as a tool to help you get unstuck and keep your eye on the prize, focusing on what you're good at, getting an assist when you need it, and letting go of the little things that are stopping you from chasing the big thing.

PART 4

THE BOLD STANDARD

Principle #13

Ask for What You Want

MY TEETH WERE CHATTERING, MY nose was bright red, and I was convinced my lips had turned blue with the cold—not a good look for attracting the attention of a major Hollywood celebrity. It was a bone-chilling -40°C night in Winnipeg, Manitoba, in mid-January 1995, and I was a nineteen-year-old kid with big hair, a big dream, and a big favor to ask the big-time actor I was waiting for by the stage door.

I was a huge music fan, and like every other teenager in those days I logged a lot of time watching the Canadian version of MTV, a music channel called MuchMusic. A spot for a new VJ had opened up, and anyone could submit a demo tape, which meant the producers at MuchMusic were going to get thousands of submissions. I knew the only way I would have any shot at all at getting an audition was if I stood out from the pack with a killer demo. I had to submit a tape so cool and so out of the ordinary that they couldn't ignore me. And even though it was minus forty, it was my lucky night!

Keanu Reeves was fresh off his blockbuster movie *Speed* and happened to be in my Canadian hometown starring in the Royal Manitoba Theatre Centre's production of *Hamlet*. (I think he wanted to test his actor chops with stage experience. Manitoba must have seemed like a safe bet!) I had no doubt that if I could somehow interview Keanu for my demo, I'd really stand out and get an audition. Which brings us back to why I was standing outside the theater about to get frostbite. As soon as Keanu exited the stage door after that night's performance, I'd make the ask.

Looking back, I know I'd been training for this bold moment for years, going back to when I was a kid and asked the manager at the Olive Garden to give me a job as a hostess. That's when I first learned that the only thing between me and what I wanted was asking. If you don't ask, you don't get. Just as important, that's also when I realized the value of posing this question to myself: *What's the worst that can happen?* If Keanu said no, or laughed in my face, or called security to get me to leave, I hadn't lost anything. And if he said yes, I'd have the coolest VJ demo tape ever made, at least by Winnipeg standards.

So there I was, shivering among the crush of girls waiting to get Keanu's autograph, when he finally emerged from the stage door. This was the moment! This was my chance! I pushed my way through the fans and media cameras to get closer to Keanu. I was just one "ask" away from my dream job as I tapped him on the shoulder.

When he turned to me, I didn't waste a second. "Keanu, can I interview you for a demo tape I need to film to get my dream job as a MuchMusic VJ?"

"You want an autograph?" he asked, giving me a confused look.

"I need your help so that I can get my dream job," I said.

"What?"

I raised my voice over the rowdy crowd. "Keanu, I want to interview you."

"Um, OK? Why don't you give me your number and I'll call you later and you can explain what it is you want?" he said.

Keanu Reeves probably made that offer to get rid of me, but I scribbled my phone number on a gum wrapper with an eyeliner pencil a girl handed me, gave it to him, and said I looked forward to hearing from him.

When word got out the next day in school about what I had done, I was mocked and ridiculed for having had the audacity to think Keanu was going to drop everything and say, "OK, strange girl. Sure, I'll do your video." The teasing went on for days. Kids I barely knew were laughing at me for believing a big Hollywood actor was going to pick up the phone and call me.

But I got the last laugh. When I got home from school four days after I left my phone number with Keanu, my mom told me a man had left two messages on the answering machine for me. *Oh my God! Keanu called and left me not one, but* two *messages!* On the second message, Keanu had left his phone number and asked me to call him back so he could help me with my demo tape!

Next thing you know, Keanu Reeves (*Keanu Reeves!*) was sitting on our living room sofa, munching Mom's chocolate chip cookies and answering my interview questions. I still have a copy of the tape to prove it! Thanks to my bold ask, and Keanu's generosity, I got the audition, though I did not get the dream job. Nevertheless, I learned a big truth about success in life: you need to ask for what you want, period.

If You Only Make One Bold Move, This Should Be It

Ask for what you want.

It sounds so simple, so basic, so obvious. But how many people ask for what they want? And how many people just live with what they get? How many people reach out only as far as they can without the risk of straining a muscle, getting hurt, or feeling embarrassed? How many people are willing to feel a little discomfort (like standing around waiting in freezing cold weather) to ask for what they want? How many people just settle? Too many.

Let's be brutally honest with each other. You know, and I know, that most people take what they get. Most people default to whatever is right in front them. Most people accept what they have, what's available to them, and acquiesce to living with whatever is comfortable and convenient.

Why ask for the raise you deserve now for the huge contribution you just made to the company's bottom line, if you can avoid that uncomfortable moment with your boss, knowing you'll still likely get some sort of bump at the end of the year?

Why go straight to the individual companies you're really interested in and asking if they have any openings, when it's so much easier to just apply for jobs posted on the giant (and impersonal) online search portals?

Why bother asking that one guy you really like if he'd want to go out sometime, versus going on dates with the guys who ask you?

Why ask a celebrity, who doesn't know you from Adam, to star in your demo reel when you can just think of a more "realistic" idea like everyone else?

Why ask? Because if you don't ask for what you want, you're not going to get it.

I'm not suggesting that you start with an extreme ask—your own version of a Keanu Moment—but if you want to, go for it! For some of you, that may feel right. But for most of you, the first step is simply to get comfortable with asking for what you want, starting with minor requests, even if it's ordering off-menu at a restaurant. Get comfortable asking for what you want, even if you start small, because that's how you develop the skills, practice the habit, and gain the confidence to ask for the *big* things in life.

Here are some tips on how to ask for what you want. I can't promise you'll be successful each time, but I do guarantee you will be much closer to getting what you want with every try.

Do Your Homework

Before approaching someone with your big ask, spend time researching who they are, what they've done, and what they're currently up to. Speaking from experience, when people ask to interview me or want my help with something, but have no clue about my background or what I am about, I'm not inclined to spend a lot of time helping them out. On the other hand, I'm far more impressed and generous with my time when I can tell someone has done their homework. If you're prepared, it shows you're focused on your goals, and you'll be taken seriously.

Build Authentic Relationships

Develop relationships where people feel invested in helping you. Showing genuine interest in the person you are speaking with is essential to building rapport. Be curious, and be a good listener.

Even if you do your homework, the secondhand information you'll collect about someone—including from their social media—generally skims the surface. It doesn't compare to hearing someone talk about themselves, their likes and dislikes, and their experiences. I love to ask people questions, which is why I love doing my podcast. And what I especially enjoy is seeing how the person I'm talking to lights up and feels good.

Showing true interest in another person makes them feel pretty darn good, and you'll benefit as well because you'll learn something. Ask questions that get beyond the surface, and really listen to the answers. Yes, the odd person may think you're being nosy or shut you down, but you don't know what will happen unless you try.

I am not a fan of small talk. It's useful when you're first getting to know someone, but it shouldn't be the whole of your conversation. Depending on your goal—whether it's a job lead or a coffee date—try to find out what makes someone tick. The weather, your latest binge-watch, and favorite restaurant recommendations are all good icebreakers, but then what? Where do you go from there?

If you already know a little about this person (you've done your homework), ease into questions beyond the details you're already familiar with. What is it about them that makes them successful? How did they get to where they are in life? What are their talents and passions, and what are their weaknesses and fears? If there is a detail about someone that sets them apart, I want to know it.

One of the most effective things you can do is to listen for things you have in common with your new acquaintance, which can immediately help to create a stronger bond. Look for ways to use common ground to maintain and strengthen your connection. Email them an interesting article you read about the topic you're both interested in, or send them a book you read, loved, and thought they'd also appreciate.

The details are what make for much richer relationships. Listen for them. And be open to sharing yours.

Be Specific

If you know what you want, ask for that one thing. Be clear, specific, and concise so that there isn't any confusion, doubt, or wiggle room in interpretation. If you're too vague and ambiguous, you're less likely to get what you're asking for. If you don't know exactly what you want, have a specific direction in mind. If you want to pivot your career from teaching to journalism, it's OK to ask for someone's perspective or advice on the best way to make that move.

I don't recommend asking if you can buy someone a cup of coffee without a specific goal in mind unless it's clear that it's just general information that you're after.

Information sessions certainly can serve a purpose. But unless you're a teenager, college student, or just starting your career, be wary of asking for anyone's time without a clear idea of exactly what you want to get out of it.

Be of Service

While the person you're asking to help you may not expect anything in return, whenever possible, think of ways to add value to their lives. Even a small but thoughtful act can go a long way to build rapport, like recommending their professional services whenever you get the chance. In return, they will likely have continued interest in helping you.

A college gymnast asked me for specific career advice. When I mentioned my kid loves gymnastics, she immediately offered to show her some cool gymnastics moves, which I really appreciated, as did my kid. Was it entirely altruistic for this young woman to make that offer? No. She wanted my help. But we both benefited from her generosity. And I'm more than happy to help her again.

What goes around comes around. Acts of kindness and service are often remembered years later, even if your gesture at the time was spontaneous with no strings attached. The person you were kind to in your twenties may reappear when you're in your forties as exactly the right person to help you get what you want. Be nice to everyone! You never know when your paths may cross again.

Check Your Tone

It's not what you say, but how you say it. People are rarely offended when you ask them for something. But if you sound entitled, you make it very difficult for anyone to want to help you. I can't stress this enough: being bold doesn't mean acting like a jerk. In fact, being lighthearted, complimentary, and even a little humble will help make anyone want to help you.

If you want to return something to the store past the return date, your chances are better if you have a friendly smile on your face, and maybe even a sense of humor about it, when you approach the sales clerk. If you act like an entitled ass, though, you can probably forget it. This is common sense, but so many people forget how far you can get just by being polite. Whether you're renegotiating your rent or asking for extra hot sauce for your tacos, your chances of getting a yes go up significantly when you treat people well—and way down if you're a jerk.

Don't Apologize

If asking for what you want feels uncomfortable, but you finally were able to flex your bold muscles and do it, I'm very proud of you! Whatever the outcome, pat yourself on the back for leaping in! But I will take back my congratulations if you immediately apologize for it. As in, "I'm sorry to bother you, but can I ask you something?"

Avoid beginning your big, bold ask with language like: "I know you're busy and I apologize for bugging you with this right now, but can I ask you . . . ?" Stop! Let's assume the person really is busy. You can show your respect for their time, but you don't have to say you're sorry. Just redo your request like this: "I know you're busy, but can I ask you something right now?" You have just removed your apology but you've acknowledged their situation.

And resist a follow-up to your ask with something like: "If not, don't worry about it. It's no big deal." That kind of talk makes it seem like you don't really feel like you deserve what you asked for, or that it's not that important to you. You're not going to get what you want if the people you ask don't think it's a big deal to you. It *is* a big deal! You are a big deal. Life is a big deal. So be bold when you ask for what you want, and don't apologize for it!

Make Your Gain Their Gain

Unfortunately, instances of helping for the sake of helping seem few and far between. The "What's in it for me?" attitude is a cultural norm, and you must acknowledge that when asking a boss or any person in a position of authority for help. When you can position your request as a victory for them as well, you may get what you want. Will it lighten their workload? Will it mean a possible promotion for them in the future? Consider what the other person might gain and use these benefits to build your case. If what you want will have a positive impact on their life too, then they will be more likely to help you get it. Help them feel invested in it. Ask for their input on your idea. Be open to their suggestions and, where possible, incorporate them into your vision.

Follow Up

Following up is an essential part of asking for what you want. And not doing it can doom your request. Many of us don't follow up, especially if we had a really hard time asking in the first place. Some of us follow up to the point of being annoying or obnoxious, which can also backfire. I can't give you a definitive answer as to how long to wait before following up and how often to send reminders, as it depends on your relationship with the person, but it's vital to close the loop.

Your follow-up technique should also take into account this person's reputation and personality (are they known for being flaky or fickle, or are they reliable and trustworthy?) as well as what is going on in their life at the moment. Are they about to take over a whole new department? Did a personal circumstance—a death, divorce, or the birth of a child— just throw their day-to-day life into disarray, and they're not responding to anyone's follow-up emails? Do they prefer texts, emails, or phone calls? Tailor your follow-up technique to fit the situation.

Let's take this scenario as an example. You own a small handmade soap business. A beauty-products influencer with a large social media following as well as some celebrity connections DMs you to say she is "#obsessed" with your "awesome-smelling soaps" and wants to order two dozen gift boxes as holiday gifts but needs them in two days for a party. You thank her and assure her you'll overnight the gift boxes so she'll have them with a day to spare. Now comes your big ask: Can she post photos and a review of your soaps and tag your business on her social media, as it will really help you get more orders for your awesome-smelling soaps? "SOOOO happy to," she writes back. "Be on the lookout for an Instagram Story as soon as I get the soaps!"

You get a notice from FedEx the following day that your customer signed for the soap delivery. But a few days pass, and while she's shared photos of the holiday party decor, she hasn't posted the pictures and review she promised you. Christmas is coming up, and this could be your biggest sales opportunity yet. It's time to follow up! Is reaching out and asking again rude? No. She said she would do it. Is asking again unprofessional? No—and you're a professional too. This is business. Is following up with her going to turn her off from ordering again? Probably not (unless she's a jerk), but it's a chance bold people take. You need those sales for your small business more than you need to worry if you're being annoying. Do it.

Give the people you ask the benefit of the doubt. I've said yes to something with the full intention of doing it that day and then totally forgot to do it. I was happy for the reminder, as I would have felt crappy for not following through on my end. And on the flip side, I've followed up with very influential people with no concerns about it. The follow-up is what can make the difference. Close the loop on asking for what you want by following up. It's just another form of asking!

If You Never Ask the Question, the Answer Is Always No

Depending on your personality, you will develop your own style for making the ask, and you'll tweak it as needed based on the circumstances. Is it urgent? How well do you know the person you're approaching? Are they difficult or receptive? Is everything on the line with this request? Lots of things will factor into your style. But if you have to boil it down to a few rules, here are the non-negotiables: don't apologize, don't be a jerk, and follow up.

Beyond that, do what works for you, and do it soon—because once you begin the bold practice of asking for what you want, you'll stop living your life by default.

Principle #14

Be Bold, Not Smart

"You've been told a lie your entire life. You've been told that being brilliant will make you successful. I'm telling you that the world doesn't favor the brilliant; it favors the bold."

THOSE ARE BOLD WORDS, CONSIDERING I had the audacity to say them to a room full of some of the smartest people on the planet—a group of MIT students, faculty, and administrators. It was November 2021, and I had been invited by the organizers of MIT's annual FAIL! Inspiring Resilience conference to speak about how I've overcome failure, and how they can too.

Why did MIT invite me? It turns out, some of their smartest students are "failing at failure"—with serious emotional and mental-health consequences—and, as luck would have it, failing is one my greatest skills. Or I should say, building the resilience to overcome failure is one of my greatest strengths. As I told the audience that day, "I may have a master's degree in failure, but I have a PhD in getting right back up again."

When you've always been at the top of your class, always praised for your straight As, no one is surprised to hear that you got accepted into a prestigious school. In fact, it's expected. Your parents are proud, your teachers are gratified, and your friends are so blasé because *of course* you got accepted into a top-tier college. *You should have won a Nobel Prize for your eleventh-grade science project, for God's sake!* they all think. At some point, being the smartest kid in the class becomes your identity.

There was a kid just like that in my high school (I'll call him Pete). He sailed through to graduation, probably smarter than many of our teachers. While Pete crushed it without trying, I had to work my ass off just to get a solid C in some classes. Nothing came easy to me, as I've said, so I learned how to be resourceful in other ways. I developed grit and resilience when I didn't get the grades I worked so hard for, and I learned to shake off the shame I felt for being sent off to the resource teacher for tutoring. And all along, I was honing my tenacity and drive to succeed, if only to prove to everyone, including myself, that failing did not mean I was a failure. But quitting would have made me a quitter.

Pete never had to learn how to get by on being scrappy or learn how to fail without falling apart. His ability to seemingly glide through school and take success for granted likely dulled his resiliency. Where I was constantly looking for ways to compensate for my weaknesses in order to succeed,

Pete and brilliant kids like him never learned how to persevere after failing.

Straight As Aren't the Answer

When it comes to getting what you want in life, it's better to be bold than brilliant. That's not to say that smart people don't succeed. Or that there aren't smart people who are also very bold. But most of us aren't Pete-level intelligent. All of us, however, can learn how to be Jennifer-level bold.

When brilliant kids like Pete get accepted to a school like MIT, it means that for the first time, their classmates, roommates, and friends are all brilliant too. Some are even more brilliant. Suddenly, the Petes are not the smartest kids in the room anymore. The same Petes who used to take pride in solving a challenging puzzle or math problem that "average" classmates struggled with are now presented with problems that aren't so simple. *They* become the struggling Jennifers, only without the resiliency and well-honed skills to help them overcome their newly revealed weaknesses. They begin to overanalyze their professors' questions, overthink the possible solutions in a bid to avoid being wrong (because they are smart and know that many things can go wrong), and can become overwhelmed with self-doubt.

Many of the high-achieving high school students who experience the shock of academic challenge and competition when they get to college are so petrified of failing that their confidence wanes while the pressure increases. This can deeply affect their emotional and mental well-being, especially if they haven't naturally developed tools to cope. To put it another way: they don't know how to fail, and you must know how to fail if you want to succeed.

When I didn't get a good grade in college, it was a little disappointing but not a catastrophe. But when a college freshman who made straight As in high school is worried about getting their first C, D, or F, they have a longer distance to fall than an average student does, and that fall can have serious consequences, even tragic ones. Some of the schools that attract the highest academic talent also have a greater-than-average campus suicide rate. In 2015, MIT took this seriously; the administration lowered class load and increased mental-health awareness and services, including programs like the FAIL! Inspiring Resilience conference, which is how I found myself at MIT speaking to a room full of brilliant kids like Pete. My job was to help students accept that it's OK to fail. And I want you to know that too.

Can't Get What You Want? Blame Your Brain

There are plenty of supersmart people who become very successful. Elon Musk, Bill Gates, Susan Wojcicki, Sheryl Sandberg, and Jeff Bezos, to name a few. Yet, there are many genius-level folks you've never heard of because their intelligence didn't translate to success. Smart people don't always get ahead; bold people do. (And incidentally, no one seems to know what happened to Pete.)

A person who has always been labeled as the "smart one" can grow up to fear rejection, like some of the students I've spoken to. They're afraid to fail because a major loss puts a question mark on their identity. Failure threatens their self-esteem. It feeds the cycle of self-doubt. Self-doubt is why people get stuck in soul-killing jobs. It's why they don't make the money they deserve. It's why they don't move forward.

Beyond being intelligent, smart people also tend to approach challenges by being well prepared. That can be a very positive trait, unless it blocks bold action—or any action at all—when you draw up lists of the pros and cons, make flowcharts, and fall into a black hole of Google searches for background research. Sometimes, it's possible to know *too* much. You can begin to look at all the things that can go wrong, which in turn can lead to analysis paralysis. Getting overly analytical about every possible decision and every potential move can make you afraid to fail, and so you don't do anything. (This is why Principle #9 is true: Naivete is a strength!) Not overanalyzing your actions and being open to taking risks can have more impact in reaching your goals. You just power through and do it.

One classic example of thinking too hard about the outcome is when a worker wants to ask for a raise. The compensation software company Payscale surveyed more than 160,000 workers who thought they deserved a salary increase. Despite the workers' belief that they'd earned a raise, two-thirds of them reported that they did not approach their supervisors, figuring they'd get a hard no. But that other third, the ones who acted with boldness? Seventy percent of those workers got the raise they asked for.

Have you overthought going after what you want? Did you freeze up and do nothing after your brain overheated while making a pro-and-con list, heavy on the cons? *Don't do it. Look at this list! You'll fail.* Maybe it was not asking for a raise, like the people in the Payscale study. Maybe you wanted to take your savings and launch your dream company—you'd be getting in on the ground floor, and the investment was solid—but then your brain came up with a "smart" dollars-and-sense argument for putting it off, or not doing it at all. Perhaps it was just a voice in your head, enumerating all the "smart" reasons why you shouldn't raise your hand in that meeting and put your idea forward, or whispering that it wasn't a "smart" move to pick up the phone and finally (finally) ask out that person you liked who seemed to like you back. *Don't do anything stupid!*

If you pause to ponder all the reasons *not* to do something, you'll be frozen in place with self-doubt and fear (those twin emotions that lead you to believe your situation is good enough as is). If acting with boldness is a good habit that will lead you to getting what you want, then overthinking is the exact opposite: a negative habit that needs to be broken.

Your smarty-pants brain means well—it's just trying to protect you from the pain of failure—but sometimes you just have to tell it to shut up. Stop thinking. Start doing. And remember that boldness, not brilliance, is what puts you on the path to success.

SLACKERS? NO, JUST BOLD

Ellen DeGeneres dropped out of the University of New Orleans after her first semester. Oprah Winfrey didn't complete college either. Her protégé, TV food star Rachael Ray, doesn't have a college degree or a formal education in the culinary arts. For that matter, neither Ray Kroc, founder of McDonald's, nor Dave Thomas, founder of Wendy's, was a high school graduate. And Kentucky Fried Chicken founder Colonel Harland Sanders didn't even make it out of elementary school. Amancio Ortega, the founder of Zara, the largest retailer in the world, left high school at age fourteen. Business mogul Richard Branson dropped out of high school at age sixteen. Motivational speaker Tony Robbins didn't go to college, and Apple cofounder Steve Jobs never graduated. Madam C. J. Walker, the founder of Madam C. J. Walker Manufacturing Company, was the first American self-made female millionaire, and the first of her siblings to be born into freedom in 1867. She had just three months of schooling.

For these bold achievers, hard work and resilience more than made up for any gaps in their formal educations. I'm not saying that you should blow off school and be a dropout. Studies repeatedly show that college graduates earn more money and are better off overall than students who don't go to college or fail to finish. I am saying, however, that being class valedictorian doesn't guarantee a rich life. Knowing how to bounce back from failure does.

To Be Successful, Get Comfortable Failing

Bold people fail. Even the boldest among us fail. *Especially* the boldest among us. And we fail often. We fail so often we plan for it. We get so comfortable with failing that failure becomes like an old, familiar friend. If you never fail, you're not chasing what you want. If you want a bigger, better, bolder life, you must accept that failure is part of the process.

Sometimes failures are so big that you feel burned and you need to take time out to recover. That's OK. A failure can feel so devasting that you take it personally; you believe *you* are the failure. But you didn't lose because you're a failure; you lost because you failed. And if you're bold, you'll know that when you're ready, you'll try again.

A bigger life doesn't happen when you sit still. A better life doesn't happen when you settle for what you're given. And a bolder life doesn't happen unless you're comfortable with failure. Most people don't lose out on what they want in life because they failed. They lose because they quit trying.

So, how do you get comfortable with failing? The same way you get comfortable with asking. You practice! Hone the skill of asking for what you want that you learned in Principle #13 . . . and get used to people slamming the door in your face, telling you no, laughing you out of the room, and doing their best to shut you down. I want you to get comfortable with failing, flopping, screwing up, blowing it, losing out, and not getting a yes.

The 10 Percent Target Principle, up next, is a master class in learning how to fail. But ultimately, it's the secret to succeeding.

Principle #15

The 10 Percent Target

WHAT DO ALL THESE FAMOUS failures have in common?

- Sir James Dyson made 5,126 design attempts at a better vacuum before designing what became the Dyson vacuum.

- Henry Ford burned through his investor funds and went bankrupt before his success with the first Ford car.

- Colonel Sanders tried more than a thousand times (1,009 to be exact) to sell his secret recipe before a restaurant bought it and put KFC in motion.

- Walt Disney was fired by a newspaper editor because "he lacked imagination and had no good ideas."

211

- The Wright brothers designed several airplanes that never, or barely, took flight before they achieved sustained lift at Kitty Hawk.

- J. K. Rowling's manuscript for the first *Harry Potter* book was rejected by twelve publishing houses, and Stephen King racked up thirty rejections for *Carrie*.

They kept trying.

If you know what you want, if you believe you can get it, if you have your road map, if you've used the *Bigger, Better, Bolder* Principles so far to get comfortable asking for things and getting a no, if you believe that failing leads to winning, then you're ready to learn about the 10 Percent Target.

Here's how it works. Practice the habit of making ten attempts at getting what you want, with the mindset that even if you miss your target 90 percent of the time, you'll be successful. By the time you make your tenth attempt, you'll hit the mark or you'll discover an even bigger, better, bolder opportunity you hadn't even thought of, until you've "failed" right into it. You probably won't even have to try ten times before you're successful. The sweet spot, I've observed, is somewhere between the fifth and tenth try.

Most people don't make ten attempts at *anything* to get what they want in life. Many don't make even *one* attempt. They convince themselves that whatever they want is impossible to attain, or they're not worthy of it, or they can't figure out a way to get it. That's why most people settle for what they have.

Then again, most people don't act with boldness. The 10 Percent Target mindset means that you're willing to get comfortable with the possibility of failing *most of the time*— nine out of ten times, in fact. But you don't give up when you miss. You try again and again, knowing that with each failure, you're only getting more resilient and bolder for the next attempt.

And here's the cool part. With every try, you're training your brain to get excited in anticipation of your next attempt. So even when you miss the target, you are rewarded with a delicious dopamine rush—the feel-good chemical that your brain releases when you're expecting a reward—just for putting in the effort. And if you succeed? You're rewarded again with a sense of accomplishment for doing what you set out to do. When you have a 10 Percent Target mindset, you're already ahead of 90 percent of the rest of the crowd.

Take Some Practice Shots—and Miss

You can tap into the 10 Percent Target anywhere and for anything.

Here's a micro lesson in how this works: cooking. For the sake of this example, I'm going to assume you are a lousy cook or that you eat a lot of takeout, because your goal is this: You want to be able to feed yourself and eat well. Your target is a great-tasting home-cooked meal. Can you roast a chicken? Whip up a salad and a perfect vinaigrette? Bake a chocolate cake? No, no, and no? Well, I'm going to bet it's because you haven't tried more than once, if at all. And if you did but your chicken burned, your salad was sad, and your cake collapsed, did you try ten times? Cooking—like asking for what you want—is a skill that you can learn, and that you have to practice. And I predict you don't have to try ten times before you are successful. As I pointed out, things start to go your way somewhere after the fifth attempt, and before the tenth.

Think of it as a numbers game—we're talking sheer volume. The more you try, the more you increase your chances for success. That's obvious, but it's absolutely shocking to me when I talk to people who try once or twice and then just give up—or who don't even try at all!

What about work? You want a raise, you did your homework, you've got your spreadsheets and your airtight reasoning, you've practiced asking for what you want, you believe in yourself . . . So you go in and ask your boss for what you want. "I can't do that for you now," she says. That's a no. You go back to your cubicle. Well, that didn't go like you thought it would . . . but . . . she left the door open a crack. "I can't do that for you *now*," she said. So you wait a month until it's "later" and ask again. Another no. You go back to your desk and stare at your computer, pondering your next move. Wait . . . what's this? She calls you in and says she can't give you a raise now, but she can offer you better assignments. A raise will only happen with a bigger title, but because you've shown how committed you are with the case you've been making—you bold thing, you—you're now first in line for a promotion. Score! By the way, extra points to you for the follow-up ask which helped push you over the line.

You can even use the 10 Percent Target in the bedroom, but let's stick with something G-rated. Your partner always leaves his socks on the floor and you grumble every time you put them in the hamper. But have you asked him to pick the damn socks up? No, not even once? Ask! Oh, you asked more than once and just resigned yourself to doing it yourself? This is one you should totally ask for ten times! Do not give up. (I'll let you decide what *else* you want to ask your partner for . . . those practice shots could be fun.)

You can use the 10 Percent Target mindset in every area of your life, even in love. But here's the thing: *You have to really want what you're shooting for.* Don't fake it. You have to believe in your goal. If you hate to cook, you're never going to roast the perfect chicken. And if you hate your job, you probably won't get a raise, much less a promotion. But if you like that person you met at the dog park last weekend and they seem to feel the same way, ask them out for coffee. Before the tenth try, maybe they'll be asking you to pick your socks up off the floor.

BOLD MOVE: MAKE A RESULTS LIST, NOT A TO-DO LIST

Instead of focusing on what you're not getting, keep a list of all the tries you've made to get it, how close you got to your target, and what you can tweak before you try again. Sometimes, you need to rest your muscles and recover before you get back out there. Change your perspective by looking at what's working, and you'll fuel your momentum.

Miss Your Tenth Shot? Here's Why You Still Win

I used the idea of the 10 Percent Target—without realizing it, before I gave it a name—when I chased what I wanted as a kid, including that Olive Garden gig and my demo tape with Keanu. I did it when I tried out for the dance troupe but wound up at the gym, which changed my whole life. I did it when I moved from Canada to LA and tried on a few jobs for size before I found a good fit for my strengths. I did it when I picked up the phone to get funding for my start-up shoe company and a few other ventures. And I did it when I wanted a network TV talk show and I wound up with my podcast instead.

Did I always get what I wanted before my tenth try? No. But here's how it worked out. Pick any one of those examples, whether it was me wanting the hostess job or the television show. I took shot after shot after shot and missed— you could even say I failed, I lost, I didn't hit my target—but then, at some point, I wound up with something even better. Every. Single. Time.

The podcast instead of trying repeatedly to work out the television deal? Perfect for me! Not getting the MuchMusic VJ gig? Great! Because that's why I eventually found myself in LA, working at 3 Arts, where I took lots of shots each day trying to fit in, but it wasn't working. Leaving 3 Arts as a result? That was ideal, because it led me to Immortal Records, which led to my fitness training business . . . and so on. I tried so hard to get into that dance group back in high school, and I missed—but that's how I wound up at the gym.

The one constant here? I never stopped taking my shots. I didn't reach my original destination, but I had my direction and ended up somewhere even better. I never settled. And that's what will happen to you, as long as you keep taking those shots.

THE BENEFITS OF BLOWING IT

- We learn something about ourselves. We notice which of our strengths need more fine-tuning. We discover weaknesses that we can either fix, forget, or farm out next time.

- We learn humility from loss and gain empathy for others who have failed.

- We learn to stretch our creative muscles. If we fail one way, we can imagine new ways to get what we want.

- We gain perspective on what we truly want. Did we *really* want that job we didn't get, or had we simply been so comfortable with the traditional career path we were on that we *assumed* it was the job we wanted?

- We become open to bigger, better opportunities we may not have imagined otherwise.

- We get the motivation we need to try even harder and come even closer to success.

- We finally see what's on the other side of *What's the worst that can happen?* and discover we've survived it.

- We have succeeded at making a bold move. Failure is a win! It means we weren't willing to settle.

Make Yourself Immune to Failure

Don't be discouraged. With every miss, you are desensitizing yourself to the sting of failure. And you're also getting closer to hitting the bull's-eye, or walking away with an even better prize.

Failing doesn't mean you're a failure. Failing means you are bold.

Principle #16

Bold Is for Life

I RECENTLY HEARD FROM A small-business owner who watched my TEDx talk, and I almost got chills when I read his words:

> My last company I started, built, and sold now has over 4,000 employees. I discovered something over the years . . . often my best employees were college athletes who were NOT starters and often only played one or two years at school. I figured they were simply used to showing up, practicing, and accepting the fact they would not start. This "habit" of showing up, trying and accepting the outcome proved to be one of the secrets of our success.

This idea of simply trying—over and over again, especially in the face of failure—is the essence of boldness. The ability to get back out there is what will save you in life, every single time.

Flaming out really hurts. Remember my superhot shoe company, NGR? It was wildly successful, until it wasn't. Everything was going beautifully. Things were humming along, and Laurence and I lined up a buyer when we were ready to turn the company over to someone who could handle the explosive growth we'd experienced. We had a signed deal . . . and then, for complex reasons, it imploded. Not only that, but I had to pay a small fortune in legal fees to clean up the mess that was left. It was a very low point in my career, a true failure, and a painful one because it struck at the core of the business I knew best, something that was part of my identity—fitness.

But pain doesn't last forever. My bank account was a little battered, as was my ego, but I also had so much to show for my efforts: a vast network of new business and media contacts, an in-depth knowledge of running a fast-growing company and managing all the moving parts, and relationships with any number of businesspeople who would eventually come back into my life when I pivoted yet again. I put a lot of time and effort into something that didn't pan out, but I connected with people I work with to this day, and I learned a ton.

Did it hurt? Hell yes. But pain is rocket fuel. You can use pain as an excuse not to try again, or you can use it to power you through to your next attempts, and that's what bold people do. The pain of failure is temporary, but the pain of regret is something else altogether.

Rejection Is Always Better Than Regret

I'm very proud of the list of acclaimed experts, authors, and celebrities I've had as guests on my *Habits & Hustle* podcast, from comedian and host Chelsea Handler to critically acclaimed author Robert Greene. But there's a short list of people I'm still dying to have on my show. And at the top of that list is actor, producer, and entrepreneur Mark Wahlberg.

Mark Wahlberg is habits and hustle personified. He is the king of discipline, known for getting up at 2:30 a.m. to work out. He structures the rest of his day in fifteen-minute increments to keep himself on point all day, every day. He ups the ante on his habits, diet, and routines depending on his latest movie role or business venture. His favorite piece of advice? "Cut the shit." That's some bold talking.

I would love the chance to ask him about his methods and his mindset, to find out how he does what he does. If it took waking up at 2:30 in the morning to work out with him, I'd do it. After all that I've shared about the power of being bold, you'd think that if I was sitting in a restaurant at a table just five feet from Mark Wahlberg, I'd turn to him and make my ask. *Hi, Mark, my name is Jennifer Cohen and . . . blah blah blah . . . would you be a guest on my podcast?*

Except, when I found myself in that exact situation one evening, I didn't make a move, much less a bold move. I simply sat there, filled with self-doubt, overthinking (there goes the brain again, getting in the way), making excuses for myself. One minute I felt too shy to say anything. The next, I thought I was too cool to bother a celebrity eating dinner at a restaurant (such an LA faux pas). I had no shortage of reasons for not asking Mark to be on the show.

My husband, who knows how much I *love* Mark Wahlberg, wondered aloud why I wasn't approaching him. My friends at the table also encouraged me. There was even a moment when Mark looked me straight in the eye and I looked back at him and . . . I promptly looked away. I did nothing. I just sat there, frozen, thinking, *What the hell are you doing? Jennifer, this was your chance! He was looking right at you!*

I tried positive distanced self-talk: *Jennifer, you can do this. This is the moment you've been waiting for. Introduce yourself and ask him to come on your damn podcast. Sure, there's only a 50 percent chance he'd say yes. OK, maybe just a 1 percent chance he'll say yes. But if you don't ask, there's a 0 percent chance he'll say yes!*

Then negative self-talk took over: *What if he says no? What if he laughs at me? I'll feel embarrassed. What if he doesn't even say a word back and instead just looks at me with pure disdain for bothering a big Hollywood star while he's trying to eat his dinner in peace?*

I yo-yoed between yes and no (limbic friction!) for the next forty-five minutes or so until I watched my dream guest get up and leave the restaurant. My heart sank. I immediately felt such deep regret. I'm still kicking myself, because this opportunity didn't slip from my fingers years ago. This happened *while I was writing this book*. It was a missed opportunity not only to have Mark on my podcast and learn from someone I so admire, but also to provide you with a rock-solid example of being bold and asking for what you want. I broke every rule I've shared with you, and I failed to take my own advice. But maybe it's not a total loss. Because you can benefit from a few things I learned the hard way.

The first and most important point is this: rejection is always better than regret. Had I asked Mark Wahlberg to be on *Habits & Hustle*, there's a chance he would have turned me down. It's possible he would have been really turned off by the fact that I interrupted his dinner, or maybe he simply wouldn't have been interested. I would have been a little embarrassed and a lot disappointed, but I would have recovered. I would have gotten over the sting of rejection much faster than the pain of regret. In general, with most things, it's much harder to get over regret. Another way to look at it is that rejection provides redirection. If you don't get one thing, you'll get something else—often something better. But if you don't try, you don't get anything, period.

The second lesson is that I forgot to ask myself a question that has propelled me forward more times than I'll ever be able to count: *What's the worst that can happen?*

It was such a rookie error. Don't ever forget to ask yourself that question! The answer will always steer you to a bold move. Sure, the more risks you take, the higher your chances of failure. But as the legendary hockey great Wayne Gretzky famously said: "You miss 100 percent of the shots you don't take."

And finally, I realized something else that night: age and time can blunt your bold edge. I'm still getting comfortable with that one, but here's the truth. When I was nineteen, I had no qualms about tapping Keanu Reeves on the shoulder and asking him to be on my demo tape. Decades later, as an accomplished woman in my own right, in my forties, I couldn't find the nerve to tap Mark Wahlberg on the arm. Self-doubt washed over me, and analysis paralysis pulled me under and finished me off. It was much easier for me to be impulsive when I was young and naive. It's harder as I've gotten older. Many of us second-guess ourselves with age, but that's when we have to remember to tap into the strength of naivete, to avoid letting age and experience get in the way.

If you're going to be afraid of something when you're chasing what you want, don't be afraid of rejection, because you can always try again. Be afraid of regret, because you'll never know what could have been. That person you didn't call back, the text you ignored, the business or career opportunity you didn't pursue . . . You weren't lazy. You were just scared of trying and failing. Don't be.

After that dinner, I learned that Wahlberg's latest movie, *Uncharted*, was slated for release. I watched the trailer and all but fell out of my chair, because the tagline was this: "Fortune favors the bold." I'm not giving up, Mark.

Life Is a Workout, So Make It a Great One

I've talked about boldness as a skill that anyone can learn, but it's also one that requires consistent practice. If you want to get fit and stay fit, you don't just reach a goal and then stop exercising and taking care of yourself. You must maintain your strength, and you may need to work even harder as time goes by to stay at that level and move beyond it. If you don't, you'll fall back to where you were before. Sometimes you need to rest your muscles along the way. You may need new equipment. You may have to change your workout. But you don't change your goal. You just change your plan.

There's a philosophy in weight training that the best way to build more muscle is to work what you have to exhaustion—to muscle failure. The idea is that you push your reps to the limit, until you fail, so that the next time you try you'll come back stronger. Something similar happens when you ask for what you want and you don't get it. With every rep, with every ask, with every chance you take when you chase what you really want, you get stronger.

And I promise you: Your life gets bigger, better, and bolder.

The 16 Principles Workbook

THIS IS YOUR BOOK, SO go ahead, write in it! Or keep a separate journal to explore these questions more fully. Either way, let your answers—and there are no wrong ones!—lead you to living your bigger, better, bolder life.

Getting to Bold

Principle #1: Strive for Bigger and Better

How will you strive for a "psychologically rich" life?

_____

_____

_____

_____

_____

_____

_____

Reflect on pages 19–20 to see the difference between people who are bold and people who are not. If the description of bold doesn't sound like you, then what is stopping you from being able to do those things?

Principle #2: Discover Your Bold Type

The more action you take to change your personality, the more your personality will change. What will you do to take more action on your goals starting *today*?

When it comes to choosing **your bold**, do you see yourself using social boldness, self-actualization boldness, or both? Why?

Build Your Bold

Principle #3: You Gotta Believe

Reflect on page 40 to see examples of tasks for bold beginners. What is the one small, bold task that you will do from start to finish today?

_____

_____

_____

_____

_____

_____

How will you become more aware of when you feel your negative self-talk is stopping you from doing what you were meant to do? How will you overcome it?

_____

_____

_____

_____

_____

_____

Principle #4: Change Your Mind

If you didn't have any fear, where would you ideally see yourself in a year from now? What limiting beliefs are standing in your way?

_____

_____

_____

_____

_____

_____

What baggage are you carrying around with you? How is it holding you back? Conversely, what luggage do you choose to carry with you? How is it helping you move forward?

_____

_____

_____

_____

_____

_____

Principle #5: Practice Bold Habits

Reflect on pages 81–84 to see the importance of gratitude. Then, think of a time you witnessed true gratitude. What was the struggle? What was the help given? How did that story impact you emotionally?

_____

_____

_____

_____

_____

What is a negative story you keep telling yourself? How can you spin it more positively?

_____

_____

_____

_____

_____

_____

Principle #6: Don't Stop Before You Start

What is a goal you've set in the past that you've stalled out on? When did you lose your motivation? What thoughts and feelings did you have around it?

_____

_____

_____

_____

_____

_____

What is one linchpin habit you can focus on today? What little things can you do to make bigger, bolder habits easier to practice?

_____

_____

_____

_____

_____

_____

Boldness Is a Skill

Principle #7: Choose a Direction, Not a Destination

When has something not gone according to plan for you? Think of a time when you didn't reach the exact goal you set out for. What happened instead? How were you redirected to something different? How did you feel about getting something other than your original goal?

_____

_____

_____

_____

_____

_____

Let's map out your future goal. Reflect on pages 123–124 to get clarity around the questions you need to ask yourself to choose a direction. What are your answers to those questions?

_____

_____

_____

_____

_____

_____

Principle #8: Be Obsessively Curious

Reflect on pages 136–137 to see how I was obsessively curious in my own life. Being obsessively curious opens up so many new doors. What is a direction you are obsessively curious about? What resources or contacts can you leverage and lean on to find out more?

_____

_____

_____

_____

_____

Meeting new people can be key to getting ahead. Where are some places you could go to find a good network? What kind of people would you like to meet?

_____

_____

_____
_____
_____
_____

Principle #9: Naivete Is a Strength

If you could magically forget any limiting beliefs or perceived obstacles to achieving a goal, what would they be? What would you do if you thought it was a sure thing? How would you go about making that goal happen?

_____
_____
_____
_____
_____
_____

You don't know what you don't know, and that can be a strength. If you didn't know the barriers to your goal, would you go for it? Would you accept a first offer? What are some things that would make you hold out for better? What standards have you developed for your goal?

_____
_____
_____
_____
_____
_____

Principle #10: Mediocrity Is a Superpower

Reflect on page 157 where I go over the difference between "Meh" and "Eh." It's all about balance. What are some weaknesses of yours that have influenced your strengths? How have you honed certain skills to compensate for other areas?

_____

_____

_____

_____

_____

_____

Conversely, what are your natural strengths? What comes easiest to you? What flourishing foundations can you continue to build on?

_____

_____

_____

_____

_____

_____

Principle #11: Bundle Your Bold

How can your natural skills and interests fill a need? What passions and talents do you have that you can market, even if you're not sure of an exact goal yet?

_____

_____

_____

_____

_____

_____

Building on those natural skills, how can you bundle them together? What skills, both professional and picked up outside of work, can work together in harmony to create new opportunities?

_____

_____

_____

_____

_____

_____

Principle #12: Fix It, Farm It Out, Forget It

Reflect on pages 179–180 to see the power of fixing something yourself. What's a small problem you have that you can fix yourself? What is unique about your skill set that lets you do so?

_____

_____

_____

_____

_____

What are you focusing on right now that isn't in service of your goals? What can you let go of right now that will free you up to focus on goal-oriented activities?

_____

_____

_____

_____

_____

The Bold Standard

Principle #13: Ask for What You Want

What are the barriers holding you back from asking for what you want? Is it a lack of connection, uncertainty, or fear of rejection? What are those obstacles and how can you overcome them?

_____

_____

_____

_____

_____

_____

What do you *really* want? Get specific. What is it on a detailed level that you need from someone?

_____

_____

_____

_____

_____

_____

Principle #14: Be Bold, Not Smart

What has made you scrappy? What have you had to work at a little harder than everyone else? How has that made a difference once you achieved a goal?

_____

_____

_____

_____

_____

_____

Think of a time when you over-thought things. What kind of outcomes did that lead to? How did that hinder your progress?

_____

_____

_____

_____

_____

_____

Principle #15: The 10 Percent Target

Think about a time when you really failed. How did you feel? What did you do next?

_____

_____

_____

_____

_____

_____

Reflect on pages 211–212 to see the failures of some of the most successful people of all time. Think about a time you tried for something over and over until you were successful. How did it feel when you finally got it? How did you adjust your strategy a little each time?

_____

_____

_____

_____

_____

_____

Principle #16: Bold Is for Life

When was the last time that failure took you by surprise? How did you react? What did you do next?

_____

_____

_____

_____

_____

_____

What is something you always wanted but never tried to get? Do you feel regret? How would your life be different if you had tried for it? As you move ahead in life, what lessons can you learn from regret?

_____

_____

_____

_____

_____

_____

If you are ready to take your boldness to the next level, make sure to visit www.biggerbetterbolderbook.com to join a mastermind group where these Principles will be overviewed and more in monthly live sessions!

References

Principle #3

Self-Efficacy

Bandura, Albert. "Self-Efficacy." In *The Corsini Encyclopedia of Psychology*, edited by I. B. Weiner and W. E. Craighead. Hoboken, NJ: Wiley, 2010. https://doi.org/10.1002/9780470479216.corpsy0836

The Batman Effect

Robson, David. "The 'Batman Effect': How Having an Alter Ego Empowers You." BBC, August 17, 2020. www.bbc.com/worklife/article/20200817-the-batman-effect-how-having-an-alter-ego-empowers-you.

White, Rachel E., Emily O. Prager, Catherine Schaefer, Ethan Kross, Angela L. Duckworth, and Stephanie M. Carlson. "The 'Batman Effect': Improving Perseverance in Young Children." *Child Development* 88, no. 5 (September–October 2017): 1563–1571. https://doi.org/10.1111/cdev.12695.

Principle #4

Fear

Saint Louis University Medical Center. "Fight Your Fears: Facing Down Anxieties Can Expand Your World." *Science-Daily*, January 29, 2016. www.sciencedaily.com/releases/2016 /01/160129171328.htm.

Negative Thinking

Nevid, Jeffrey S. "Is Your Brain on Automatic Pilot?" *Psychology Today*, March 4, 2018. www.psychologytoday.com/us/blog /the-minute-therapist/201803/is-your-brain-automatic-pilot.

Principle #5

Gratitude Stories

Huberman, Andrew D. "The Science of Gratitude and How to Build a Gratitude Practice." *Huberman Lab*. Podcast audio. November 22, 2021. https://hubermanlab.com/the-science-of -gratitude-and-how-to-build-a-gratitude-practice.

Mindfulness

Kiken, Laura G., and Natalie J. Shook. "Does Mindfulness Attenuate Thoughts Emphasizing Negativity, but Not Positivity?" *Journal of Research in Personality* 53 (December 2014): 22–30. https://doi.org/10.1016/j.jrp.2014.08.002.

Singh, Yogesh, Arun Goel, Rajesh Kathrotia, and Prashant M. Patil. "Role of Yoga and Meditation in the Context of Dysfunctional Self: A Hypothetico-Integrative Approach." *Advances in Mind-Body Medicine* 28, no. 3 (August 2014): 22–25.

Self-Hypnosis

Jiang, Heidi, Matthew P. White, Michael D. Greicius, Lynn C. Waelde, and David Spiegel. "Brain Activity and Functional Connectivity Associated with Hypnosis." *Cerebral Cortex* 27, no. 8 (August 2017): 4083–5093.

Decision-Making

Sollisch, Jim. "The Cure for Decision Fatigue." *Wall Street Journal,* June 10, 2016. www.wsj.com/articles/the-cure-for-decision-fatigue-1465596928.

Principle #10

Identifying Strengths

Flade, Peter, Jim Asplund, and Gwen Elliot. "Employees Who Use Their Strengths Outperform Those Who Don't." Gallup, October 8, 2015. www.gallup.com/workplace/236561/employees-strengths-outperform-don.aspx.

Steimer, Andreas, and André Mata. "Motivated Implicit Theories of Personality: My Weaknesses Will Go Away, but My Strengths Are Here to Stay." *Personality and Social Psychology Bulletin* 42, no. 4 (April 2016): 415–429. https://doi.org/10.1177/0146167216629437.